An Orthodox Catechism

Hercules Collins

Edited and Introduced by

Michael A. G. Haykin and
G. Stephen Weaver, Jr.

RBAP
Palmdale, CA

Copyright © 2014 Michael A. G. Haykin and G. Stephen Weaver, Jr. Applies to "Introduction." All rights reserved.

Requests for information should be sent to:

RBAP
349 Sunrise Terrace
Palmdale, CA 93551
rb@rbap.net
www.rbap.net

No part of this publication may be reproduced, stored in a retrieval system, or transmitted in any way by any means, electronic, mechanical, photocopy, recording, or otherwise, without the prior permission of RBAP except as provided by USA copyright law, catechism excepted.

Printed in the United States of America.

Cover design by Kalós Grafx Studios | www.kalosgrafx.com

Formatted for print by Cameron Porter.

ISBN 978-0-9802179-1-9

Hercules Collins' *An Orthodox Catechism* is an important work that is worthy of the attention of modern Baptists. Collins' Baptist emendations to the Heidelberg Catechism resulted in a document that retains all of the first-person warmth and Christ-centered instruction of that older, more widely known document. I am glad to see this work in print (especially with the helpful introductory material) and commend it to Baptists everywhere.

Tom Ascol
Founders Ministries
****

This is a much-needed and timely publication of an old catechism. *An Orthodox Catechism* (a seventeenth-century English Particular or Calvinistic Baptist document) shows fundamental continuity with both Protestant orthodoxy and the catholic tradition of historic Christianity. The document itself shows this as does the fine introduction by Drs. Haykin and Weaver. Collins wrote this as a pastor, desiring that his flock be "better established, strengthened, and settled on" truth and protected from "every wind and blast, every puff and breath of Error, and Heresie." *An Orthodox Catechism* is, as the author says, an "Epitome of Law and Gospel, suited to every ones capacity in God's House…" and "Milk for Babes, and Meat for strong Men." May it strengthen many churches!

Richard C. Barcellos
Grace Reformed Baptist Church
Palmdale, CA
****

There was a time when Baptist Christians regularly used catechisms in their homes and local churches. Often Baptists wrote their own catechisms, though they also periodically revised paedobaptist catechisms that were otherwise sound. One famous Reformed catechism, the Heidelberg Catechism, was important enough to be revised by Hercules Collins in 1680 for the use of his fellow Baptists. Contemporary Baptist advocates of catechisms owe Michael Haykin and Steve Weaver a debt of gratitude for making *An Orthodox Catechism* available once again. May it gain a wide usage in our families and in churches.

Nathan A. Finn
Associate Professor of Historical Theology
Southeastern Baptist Theological Seminary
****

Hercules Collins' revision of the Heidelberg Catechism is one of the most valuable and least-known resources in the history of Particular Baptist spirituality. *An Orthodox Catechism* (1680) combines the vitality of Continental Protestant piety with the clarity of New Testament churchmanship, and invites its readers into those spiritual and theological traditions which will do most to inform our minds, warm our hearts, and shape our practice.

Crawford Gribben
Professor of Early Modern British History
Queen's University Belfast
****

There are few compositions in the history of the Christian church as perspicuous, edifying, and beautiful as the

Heidelberg Catechism. It was a deft stroke of denominational ecumenicity when Hercules Collins adapted that catechism for Baptist life. Now *An Orthodox Catechism,* as Collins named it, is being reprinted with helpful and scholarly introductory material by Michael Haykin, Jim Renihan, and Steve Weaver. I will personally give a hearty welcome to this book and am grateful for its availability. For history, theology, and spiritual nourishment this should be a book of choice.

Thomas J. Nettles
Professor of Historical Theology
The Southern Baptist Theological Seminary
****

Table of Contents

Acknowledgements i

Preface by Hercules Collins 1

Foreword by James M. Renihan 7

Introduction by Michael A. G. Haykin and G. Stephen Weaver, Jr. 9

1. General Introduction and The First Part: Of Man's Misery 41

2. The Second Part: Of Man's Redemption (Introductory Questions) 47

3. The Second Part: Of Man's Redemption (God the Father) 53

4. The Second Part: Of Man's Redemption (God the Son) 57

5. The Second Part: Of Man's Redemption (God the Holy Spirit) 67

6. The Second Part: Of Man's Redemption (The Sacraments) 73

7. The Second Part: Of Man's Redemption (Baptism) 75

8. The Second Part: Of Man's Redemption (The Lord's Supper) 83

9. The Third Part: Of Man's Thankfulness (Introductory Questions) 91

10. The Third Part: Of Man's Thankfulness (The Law of God) 95

11. The Third Part: Of Man's Thankfulness (Prayer) 109

12. The Nicene and Athanasian Creeds 117

Acknowledgements

In this new edition of *An Orthodox Catechism*, we have sought to retain the original formatting as much as possible. Original spelling, punctuation, and some wording have been changed for the modern reader. We have added numbering in order to make referencing particular questions easier. We have also corrected the more obvious printer's errors and typos. The headings we added (though slightly modified) come from the edition of the *Heidelberg Catechism* contained in Philip Schaff, *The Creeds of Christendom: Volume III, The Evangelical Protestant Creeds*, Grand Rapids: Baker Books, 1996. We also chose not to print two sections from the original edition. The questions that dealt with the laying on of hands after baptism were deleted, as was the appendix on hymn-singing. Since we desire this catechism to be useful to churches in our day, we felt that these sections might detract from our goal.

A special word of appreciation is due to Enrique Durán, Jr., who did the initial transcription of the catechism and assisted in proofreading.

The Editors

Preface[1]

Unto the church of Christ, who upon confession of faith have been baptized, meeting in Old Gravel Lane, London. Grace, mercy, and peace be multiplied unto you, and the good will of Him which dwelt in the bush be with your spirits, Amen.

Dearly Beloved,
Forasmuch as there is but a small time allotted unto any of us in this world, and not knowing but my staff stands next to the door ready to depart, I am desirous in this respect so to bestow my precious and present time in my Lord's business, as I may not return to him with my talent wrapped up in a napkin, but may leave behind me some poor token and testimony of my love and duty towards Him, and His blessed spouse the Church.

And forasmuch as the day we live in is very gloomy and dark, full of error and heresy, which spreads more and more (through the indefatigable endeavors of the maintainers of it) like an overflowing leprosy, and eats as does a canker.

Also considering it is a day of great declension in love to God and one to another also, from those gospel truths, the least of which is more worth than our lives: all which may give God just cause to say to England's professors, as once to Israel, "What iniquity have your fathers found in Me that they are gone away far from Me?" As if God should say, "Am I not the same as ever in power, goodness, faithfulness? Is not My word and ordinances the same, yea, My promises and heaven the same now as ever?"

---

[1] Collins' original preface is printed here with minor alterations.

Now that you may not be shaken, shattered, and carried away with every wind and blast, every puff and breath of error, and heresy; also that you may be the better established, strengthened, and settled on that sure rock and foundation of salvation, Christ's merits, in opposition to the poor imperfect works of an impotent creature; also settled on the foundation of church-constitution, on which you are already built, through the grace of God which stirred you up to search the divine oracle, and rule of Divine service, as Ezra and Nehemiah searched into the particular parts of God's worship, by which means they came to the practice of that almost lost ordinance of God, the Feast of Tabernacles, which for many years was not practiced after the due order, though a general notion was retained about it; I say, under these considerations, I have in charitable regard to your souls, presented you with this small (but I am bold to say) sound piece of divinity, which may not unsuitably be styled an abridgment, or epitome of law and gospel, suited to everyone's capacity in God's house. Here is milk for babes, and meat for strong men. It may not unsuitably be compared to the waters of the sanctuary, where some may go up to the ankles, others to the knees, others to the loins, and they are deep enough for others to swim in. Here you are not only taught to be good Christians, but good moralists, the wane of which among them that have the leaves and lamps of profession (as it is to be feared such have little more) is of a heart-breaking consideration to many that desire to walk with God.

Now albeit here may be many things which some of you may know already, yet unto such those things I hope will be acceptable as St. Peter's epistles were to the scattered saints, though they knew much of the matter before, yet I dare say here is some things which may be for information as well as establishment to the most knowing among you.

I have not undertaken to present you with new notions or principles, hoping an Athenian spirit is in none of you, but do believe that an old gospel (to you that have tasted the sweetness of it) will be more acceptable than a new, though published by an angel from heaven.

In what I have written you will see I concenter with the most orthodox divines in the fundamental principles and articles of the Christian faith, and also have industriously expressed them in the same words, which have on the like occasion been spoken, only differing in some things about church-constitution, wherein I have taken a little pains to show you the true form of God's house, with the coming in thereof, and the going out thereof. But I hope my zeal in this will not be misinterpreted by any that truly fear God. That God whom we serve is very jealous of his worship; and forasmuch as by His providence the law of His house has been preserved and continued to us, we look upon it as our duty in our generation to be searching out the mind of God in His holy oracle, as Ezra and Nehemiah did the Feast of Tabernacles, and to reform what is amiss, as Hezekiah, who took a great deal of pains to cleanse the house of God, and set all things in order, that were out of order, particularly caused the people to keep the Passover according to the institution. For it had not, says the text, been of a long time kept in such sort as it was written. And albeit the pure institutions of Christ were not for some hundreds of years practiced according to the due order, or very little through the innovations of antichrist; and as circumcision for about forty years was unpracticed in the wilderness, yet as Joshua puts this duty in practice as soon as God signified His mind in that particular, so we having our judgments informed about the true way of worship, do not dare to stifle the light God has given us.

Now albeit there are some differences between many godly divines and us in church constitution, yet inasmuch as those things are not the essence of Christianity, but that we do agree in the fundamental doctrine thereof, there is sufficient ground to lay aside all bitterness and prejudice, and labor to maintain a spirit of love each to other, knowing we shall never see all alike here. We find in the primitive times that the baptism of Christ was not universally known. Witness the ignorance of Apollos that eminent disciple and minister, which knew only the baptism of John. And if God shall enlighten any into any truth, which they shall stifle for base and unwarrantable ends, know that it is God who must judge, and not man. And wherein we cannot concur, let us leave that to the coming of Christ Jesus, as they did their difficult cases in the Church of old until there did arise a priest with Urim and Thummin, that might certainly inform them of the mind of God thereabout.

I have proposed three creeds to your consideration, which ought thoroughly to be believed and embraced by all those that would be accounted Christians, viz. the Nicene Creed, Athanasian Creed, and the Creed commonly called the Apostles. The last of which contains the sum of the gospel, which is industriously opened and explained. And I beseech you do not slight it because of its form, nor antiquity, nor because supposed to be composed by men; neither because some that hold it maintain some errors, or whose conversation may not be correspondent to such fundamental principles of salvation. But take this for a perpetual rule, that whatever is good in any, owned by any, whatever error or vice it may be mixed withal, the good must not be rejected for the error or vice sake, but owned, commended, and accepted. Here is also in the close of the book a brief, but full exposition of that prayer Christ taught His disciples. Also, the Decalogue, or Ten Commandments, unfolded.

Now forasmuch as I have taken a great deal of pains in gathering these broken fragments together for your utility and profit, I hope you will take a little pains to read it, and more to live it; and I pray do it seriously and observingly. Read it humbly and frequently, read it with prayer and meditation, then am I sure thou who art a true Christian will love it more and more. And as you love your own souls, love your children's, and declare it in praying for them, as Job did for his, and instructing them, as Abraham did his, also winning them to good by a good example. And that this book may be of advantage to youth as well as others, it is catechistically handled for their easier learning the principles of the Christian religion, that so they being seasoned with the true articles of Christian faith, may not so easily be tainted with the sentiments of men of corrupt minds in time of temptation. And it is heartily desired that parents, especially professing ones, were more concerned for the everlasting welfare of their children, as David was for Solomon, when he charged him near his death to keep the commandments and judgments of God above all. And if parents would but conscientiously read those Divine oracles which hold forth their duty to their children, it would doubtless be to them of great advantage.

As for this that I have presented to public view, I beg the reader's kind indulgence as to the faults escaped therein. And for those whom the Lord has committed to my charge, that the eternal God may be your refuge, and underneath you everlasting arms; that grace may be opened to your hearts, and your hearts to grace; that the blessing of the God of Abraham, Isaac, and Jacob may be upon you, and the eternal Spirit may be with you, shall be the prayer of your unworthy brother, but more unworthy pastor,

H.C

Foreword

James M. Renihan

Perhaps the best loved confessional statement of the sixteenth century, the *Heidelberg Catechism* has provided 'comfort in life and in death' to generations of godly Christians in the Dutch churches. Though quite explicitly written from within the paedobaptist tradition, its beautiful devotional language and precise expressions of the deep things of Christian faith have been loved in many different ecclesiastical communions. Few today realize that it has served an important role in the lives of Baptists.

In the past two decades, post-Reformation scholastic theology has been enjoying a period of re-assessment from scholars, leading to growing appreciation for the quality and content of the work produced during this era. The *Heidelberg Catechism* stands as a monument to the excellence of theology in this period. Exact doctrinal statements, couched in deeply devotional language, demonstrate the practical importance of theology for the lives of believers. Recognizing this fact, Hercules Collins took these statements and adapted (or perhaps supplemented) them to accord with his own convictions of believer's baptism. The end result is a wonderful, practical, and helpful statement for Baptist churches.

Collins, a leading pastor among the seventeenth-century English Particular Baptists, understood the potential benefits of the *Heidelberg Catechism* for the people under his pastoral care. In order to provide them with an accessible version within his own system of church practice, he edited the Heidelberg and published it in 1680 under the title *An Orthodox Catechism*.

Many are familiar with its structure, summarized by the words, 'Guilt, Grace and Gratitude.' It exposes our sinfulness, points us to the rich grace of God in Jesus Christ, and teaches us both the motive and method of showing our thankfulness to our Lord. As a good catechism, it summarizes the most important aspects of the Christian life.

This *Orthodox Catechism* is really the second of three important late seventeenth-century works which tie English Baptists to the post-Reformation era. The first is the *Second London Confession*, first published in 1677, a revision of the *Westminster Confession of Faith* of 1648 and the *Savoy Declaration* of 1658. The third is the *Baptist Catechism* of 1693, an edited version of the *Shorter Catechism* of the Westminster Assembly, first published in 1647. Together these three documents may provide something of 'Three Forms of Unity' for Baptist churches.

We must express our thanks to Michael Haykin and Steve Weaver for their labors in bringing this work back into public view. It ought to be used in churches, Bible classes, Christian schools, home schools, and in families. Children raised on the sound doctrine of the *Orthodox Catechism* will have a basis for a godly life that will stay with them throughout their lives. Churches that adopt this catechism as a teaching tool will provide their people with a full system of Christian theology, a solid foundation for both faith and godliness. Perhaps the *Orthodox Catechism* will become one of the best loved confessional statements of the twenty-first century in Baptist churches. What a blessing that would be!

Introduction

Michael A. G. Haykin and G. Stephen Weaver, Jr.*

To "concenter with the most orthodox divines":
Hercules Collins and his *An Orthodox Catechism*
—a slice of the reception history of the Heidelberg Catechism

Just over a hundred and fifteen years after the publication of the first edition of the Heidelberg Catechism in 1563, Hercules Collins (1646/7-1702)–the third pastor of the oldest Particular (that is, Calvinistic) Baptist congregation in Great Britain–published a baptistic edition of the Heidelberg Catechism (HC) in 1680 that he entitled *An Orthodox Catechism* (OC).[1] He

---

* Michael A. G. Haykin is the professor of church history and biblical spirituality at The Southern Baptist Theological Seminary, Louisville, Kentucky, and the Director of the Andrew Fuller Center for Baptist Studies (at Southern Seminary). G. Stephen Weaver, Jr. (Ph.D., The Southern Baptist Theological Seminary) is pastor of Farmdale Baptist Church in Frankfort, KY. He is also research assistant to Dr. Michael A. G. Haykin for the Andrew Fuller Center for Baptist Studies. His dissertation focused on the seventeenth-century English Baptist Hercules Collins. Along with Michael Haykin, Steve co-edited, *"Devoted to the Service of the Temple": Piety, Persecution, and Ministry in the Writings of Hercules Collins* (Reformation Heritage Books, 2007).

[1] Hercules Collins, *An Orthodox Catechism: Being the Sum of Christian Religion, Contained in the Law and the Gospel. Published for preventing the Canker and Poison of Heresy and Error* (London, 1680). For a comparison of the HC and the OC, see James M. Renihan, ed., *True Confessions: Baptist Documents in the Reformed Family* (Owensboro, KY: Reformed Baptist Academic Press, 2004), 231-87, which places edited versions of the OC and the HC side by side so as to identify changes, both major and minor, as well as additions. For accuracy Renihan's edition has been compared with the original printing of OC listed above and the HC as contained in Zacharias Ursinus, *The Summe of Christian*

did so with a deep sense of the valuable role that this catechism could play in both refuting serious doctrinal error and deepening the love of God's saints for God and one another, since, in Collins' opinion, his was a day of "great declension" on both counts.[2] Collins' day was also a time of intense persecution for anyone who sought to worship outside of the state church, the Church of England. Nearly the totality of that body of Christians known as the Puritans, who had sought a greater reformation of the state church for a hundred years or so, had been forced out of the Church of England eighteen years earlier in 1662. Various pieces of legislation, collectively known as the Clarendon Code (1661-1665), subsequently made all but Anglicans second-class citizens. In fact, between 1660 and 1688, the Puritan cause was

---

Religion, trans. D. Henry Parry (London: James Young, 1645). This edition, according to James Renihan "is obviously the edition used by Collins" (*True Confessions*, 236).

The spelling in quotations from seventeenth-century texts within this essay has generally been modernized, as has the use of capitals. The term "concenter," used in the quote in the title, is sometimes spelled "concentre." It is here used with the meaning of being in accord with or in harmony with "the most orthodox divines." The quote is taken from Collins, "Preface" to *Orthodox Catechism*, [iv]; Renihan, *True Confessions*, 237. In referencing Collins' version of the HC, the pagination of the original will be noted, then the Renihan edition.

The congregation of which Collins was the pastor is still in existence today as the oldest Baptist church in the world. For the history of the church, see Ernest F. Kevan, *London's Oldest Baptist Church: Wapping 1633–Walthamstow 1933* (London: Kingsgate Press, 1933) and Robert W. Oliver, *From John Spilsbury to Ernest Kevan: The Literary Contribution of London's Oldest Baptist Church* (London: Grace Publications Trust for The Evangelical Library, 1985).

[2] Collins, "Preface" to *Orthodox Catechism*, [i–iii]; Renihan, *True Confessions*, 236-37.

a "church" under the cross.[3] The state actively harassed those outside the established church and imprisoned their leaders. In the words of Gerald R. Cragg, "They were harried in their homes and in their meeting houses; they were arrested, tried and imprisoned. A few were transported; many died."[4]

Like other Nonconformist ministers during this time, Collins knew personally what it meant to suffer at the hands of state officials. During the first half of Collins' pastoral ministry (from March 23, 1676, when he was set aside as "an overseer or an elder"[5] until the Act of Toleration in 1689) the congregation had to meet in secret for fear of persecution. Collins himself was imprisoned for his nonconformity in 1684. Given the persecution that the Baptists faced in this period, it should come as no surprise that Collins chose the HC for the basis of his catechism since it was, as Mark Noll has stated, "a superb statement of faith for a persecuted people. Its stress, from the very first question, on God's desire to comfort his own, as well as its emphasis on the transcendent goodness of God's providence, brought reassurance to those who felt that they had been abandoned by all earthly powers."[6]

In what follows, this slice of the reception history of the HC by a Reformed, albeit non-paedobaptist, community is

---

[3] For an excellent study of this era of Puritanism, see Gerald R. Cragg, *Puritanism in the Period of the Great Persecution 1660–1688* (Cambridge: University Press, 1957). See also Michael R. Watts, *The Dissenters. Volume 1: From the Reformation to the French Revolution* (Oxford: Clarendon Press, 1978), 221-62.

[4] Cragg, *Puritanism in the Period of the Great Persecution*, vii.

[5] Kevan, *London's Oldest Baptist Church*, 38.

[6] Mark A. Noll, *Confessions and Catechisms of the Reformation* (Vancouver, British Columbia: Regent College Publishing, 2004), 135.

12 | *An Orthodox Catechism*

examined in order to see how an influential Baptist/Puritan pastor adapted the catechism for his community in the late seventeenth century. First, though, it is needful to say something about Collins himself.

A biographical sketch

Although Collins was the author of some dozen works written between the years 1680 and his death in 1702, very little is really known about his early years.[7] According to John Piggott (d.1713), the pastor of Little Wild Street Baptist Church in London and who preached Collins' funeral sermon, a keen interest in Christianity showed itself early in Collins' life, which probably indicates that his parents were Christians.[8] If his parents were believers, the fact that they gave their son the name of a pagan Greek hero is odd, to say

---

[7] Sketches of Collins' life have been largely dependent on the sparse biographical remarks made at Collins' funeral by John Piggot: *A Sermon Preached at the Funeral of The Reverend Mr. Hercules Collins, Late Minister of the Gospel* (London: A. Bell and J. Baker, 1702), 33-36. For such dependence, see Thomas Crosby, *The History of the English Baptists* (London, 1740), III, 129-30; Joseph Ivimey, *A History of the English Baptists* (London, 1814), II, 435-38; *idem*, *A History of the English Baptists* (London: B.J. Holdsworth, 1823), III, 301-06.

For recent studies of the life of Collins, see Michael A. G. Haykin, "The Piety of Hercules Collins (1646/7–1702)" in his and Steve Weaver, eds., *Devoted to the Service of the Temple: Piety, Persecution, and Ministry in the Writings of Hercules Collins* (Grand Rapids: Reformation Heritage Books, 2007), 1-30. See also Michael A. G. Haykin, "Collins, Hercules (d. 1702)" in H. C. G. Matthew and Brian Harrison, eds., *Oxford Dictionary of National Biography* (Oxford: Oxford University Press, 2004), s.v. and his chapter "Hercules Collins and the Art of Preaching" in his *A Cloud of Witnesses: Calvinistic Baptists in the 18th Century* (Darlington, England: Evangelical Times, 2006), 21-26.

[8] Piggott, *Mr. Hercules Collins*, 33.

Introduction | **13**

the least![9] This curious naming, though, may well be linked to the fact that the name of Hercules was renowned for his great feats of strength and heroism. Possibly, Collins' parents were hoping that their son would do great exploits for Christ. If so, they would not have been disappointed, for, in his day, Collins was among the most distinguished London ministers of the Calvinistic Baptist denomination.[10]

By the late 1660s Collins had become serious about his commitment to Christ and would later recall how it was during this period of time he began to know the reality of spiritual warfare.[11] There is also good evidence that by the middle of the following decade Collins was a member of Petty France Particular Baptist Church in London.[12] If so, he might have received some pastoral training in this congregation, where the pastors, from September 1675

---

[9] The name is found among other Puritans as well. For instance, one of the men involved in the execution of Charles I in 1649 was a colonel by the name of Hercules Hunks. See Geoffrey Robertson, *The Tyrannicide Brief. The Story of the Man Who Sent Charles I to the Scaffold* (New York: Pantheon Books, 2005), 195, 275, 281, and 329.

[10] Along with Hanserd Knollys (1599-1691) and William Kiffin (1616-1701), and three other Baptist leaders, Collins is described as one of those Baptist ministers at the close of the seventeenth century who was "eminent for…usefulness" in their denomination (Ivimey, *History of the English Baptists*, III, 46).

[11] Hercules Collins, "The Epistle Dedicatory" to *Three Books: Viz. I. The Scribe instructed unto the Kingdom of Heaven. II. Mountains of Brass: Or, A Discourse upon the Decrees of God. III. A Poem on the Birth, Life, Death, Resurrection and Ascension of our Lord and Saviour Jesus Christ* (London, 1696), iii-iv, 33-34.

[12] W. T. Whitley, *The Baptists of London 1612-1928* (London: Kingsgate Press, [1928]), 104; Murdina D. MacDonald, "London Calvinistic Baptists, 1689-1727: tensions within a dissenting community under toleration" (D.Phil. thesis, Regent's Park College, University of Oxford, 1982), 317-18.

14 | *An Orthodox Catechism*

onwards, were William Collins (d.1702), who had had university training, and Nehemiah Coxe (d.1689).[13] William Collins and Coxe were probably the authors behind the Second London Confession of Faith (1677/1689), that most important of all Baptist confessional documents.[14]

Hercules Collins' first and only pastoral charge was the Particular Baptist Church in Wapping, London. Collins was appointed pastor of this work on March 23, 1677.[15] Here he would have a fruitful ministry. Roughly ten years into his ministry, the Church numbered around 140 members, and by the time of his death in 1702, the membership of the church had doubled.[16] Much of the context in which this church growth took place, though, was one of state harassment and outright violence, as has been noted. And the final years of the reign of Charles II (r.1660–1685) saw an intensification of this persecution. During this period of time nearly 4,000 London Dissenters were arrested or convicted for being present at what the state regarded as illegal religious meetings.[17] The meetinghouse of Collins' congregation was attacked at least once during this period of time, with the pulpit and pews being destroyed and windows smashed.[18] In the summer of 1683 Collins was cited for failure to attend his

---

[13] T. E. Dowley, "A London Congregation during the Great Persecution: Petty France Particular Baptist Church, 1641–1688", *The Baptist Quarterly*, n.s. 27 (1977–1978), 234.

[14] Dowley, "London Congregation", 234.

[15] Kevan, *London's Oldest Baptist Church*, 38.

[16] MacDonald, "London Calvinistic Baptists", 336-37.

[17] Tim Harris, *London Crowds in the Reign of Charles II: Propaganda and Politics from the Restoration until the Exclusion Crisis* (Cambridge: Cambridge University Press, 1987), 485.

[18] Ivimey, *History of the English Baptists*, II, 448-49.

local parish church. The following year he was actually imprisoned in Newgate Prison under the provisions of the Five Mile Act (1665), which forbade Nonconformist preachers and pastors to live within "five miles of any city or town or borough."[19] A defense of Dissent that Collins had penned two years earlier, *Some Reasons for Separation From the Communion of the Church of England, and the Unreasonableness of Persecution Upon that Account*, may well have been a factor in his imprisonment.[20] In this tract, Collins clearly argued that the use of force by the state can never bring about the spiritual enlightenment that lies at the heart of Christianity–"that is God's work alone" and "God's gift."[21]

Newgate was the most notorious prison in seventeenth-century England. Destroyed by the Great Fire of London in 1666, it was soon rebuilt by 1672. The new prison was not much better, though, than the one it replaced. The cells were dark, damp, poorly ventilated, and frequently overcrowded with prisoners. In the heat of summer the stench of Newgate was appalling. The colder weather would have been equally difficult since the cells did not have fireplaces. In such conditions, there were frequent, virulent outbreaks of typhus and other water-borne and air-borne diseases. The novelist Henry Fielding (1707–1754) well captured the horror of imprisonment in Newgate when he termed it a "prototype of

---

[19] Piggott, *Mr. Hercules Collins*, 33.
[20] MacDonald, "London Calvinistic Baptists", 316-17.
[21] *Some Reasons for Separation From the Communion of the Church of England, and the Unreasonableness of Persecution Upon that Account* (London: John How, 1682), 14.

16 | *An Orthodox Catechism*

hell."[22] Not surprisingly, a number of those Dissenters imprisoned in the prison during this time did not survive the ordeal.[23] At least three of Collins' fellow Baptists who were with him in Newgate prison perished there: Francis Bampfield (1614/15–1684)–a Seventh-day Baptist with "an intensely personal piety and a commitment to practical Christianity"[24]–Thomas Delaune (d.1685), an Irish Baptist,[25] and Zachariah Ralphson (d.1684), described by the eighteenth-century Baptist historian Joseph Ivimey (1773–1834) as "a person of considerable learning and usefulness."[26] After the deaths of Bampfield and Ralphson, Collins wrote a funeral sermon for them in which he expressed something of the horrors he saw in prison: men of "threescore, fourscore years of age"–Bampfield was close to seventy at the time of his arrest–"hurried to prison for nothing else but for worshipping their God."[27]

Having been released, Collins led his congregation in the summer of 1687 to move to another London location. The

---

[22] Cited "Newgate" (http://www.ludgatecircus.com/newgate.htm; accessed May 23, 2007).

[23] John Coffey, *Persecution and Toleration in Protestant England, 1558–1689* (Harlow, Essex: Pearson Education Ltd., 2000), 174-77.

[24] Richard L. Greaves, " 'Making the Laws of Christ His Only Rule': Francis Bampfield, Sabbatarian Reformer" in his *Saints and Rebels: Seven Nonconformists in Stuart England* (Macon, Georgia: Mercer University Press, 1985), 210. On Bampfield, see Greaves, "Francis Bampfield, Sabbatarian Reformer" in his *Saints and Rebels*, 179-210.

[25] See Michael A.G. Haykin, "Delaune, Thomas (d.1685)", in Matthew and Harrison, eds., *Oxford Dictionary of National Biography, s.v.*

[26] *A History of the English Baptists* (London, 1811), I, 405.

[27] *Counsel for the Living, Occasioned from the Dead: Or, A Discourse on Job III.17,18. Arising from the Deaths of Mr. Fran. Bampfield and Mr. Zach. Ralphson* (London, 1684), 15.

congregation erected a new building for worship on James Street in Stepney. The boldness of the move–religious toleration had not yet been declared in England and Wales–speaks volumes about the vigorous leadership that Collins exercised both within his own church and in the larger Calvinistic Baptist community of London. Although the building had to be expanded shortly after it was built because of the numbers attending worship, the congregation met on this site for the next forty-three years.[28]

The reign of the Roman Catholic James II (r.1685–1688), who had succeeded Charles II, came to a quick end in 1688, when a coup d'état occurred, placing the firmly Protestant William III (r.1688–1702) and his wife Mary II (r.1688–1692)–the daughter of James II–on the throne. Within a year of their accession the Toleration Act was passed. Although this act did not secure total religious freedom–Dissenters remained very much second-class citizens and the Church of England clearly remained without rival as the state church–it did end the overt persecution of the previous thirty years or so.[29]

In this new political reality, Calvinistic Baptist leaders in London called for a general assembly of Baptists to meet in the capital. It was this assembly that gave official sanction to the confessional document known as the Second London Confession of Faith, also known as The 1689 Confession. This

---

[28] Kevan, *London's Oldest Baptist Church*, 48.

[29] See James E. Bradley, "Toleration, Nonconformity, and the Unity of the Spirit: Popular Religion in Eighteenth-Century England" in his and Richard A. Muller, eds., *Church, Word, and Spirit: Historical and Theological Essays in Honor of Geoffrey W. Bromiley* (Grand Rapids: William B. Eerdmans Publ. Co., 1987), 183–185 for a brief summary of the impact of the Act of Toleration.

would become the doctrinal standard for the British Calvinistic Baptist community well into the nineteenth century and also stands behind many of the confessional texts of American Baptist life. Collins' name was the fifth on the list of signators, a list that was headed by those of Knollys and Kiffin.[30]

During the 1690s Collins became an increasingly respected figure within the London Baptist community, fueled in part by the growing body of his published works.[31] His first written work had been the Baptist adaptation of the HC. In the decade following the 1689 assembly, he wrote a number of works defending the particulars of Baptist ecclesial polity. According to the early eighteenth-century Baptist historian Thomas Crosby (1683–c.1751), Collins did not enjoy the advantage of a learned education.[32] Yet, as his theological works reveal, there is little doubt that he was well versed in theology. Piggott speaks of his doctrinal convictions as being "agreeable to the sentiments of the Reformed Churches in all fundamental articles of faith" and of his habitual use of spiritual conversation with friends as a way of growing as a Christian.[33]

By the time that Collins died on October 4, 1702, he was regularly preaching to an audience of roughly 700 people, which would have made his congregation one of the largest

---

[30] William L. Lumpkin, *Baptist Confessions of Faith* (Rev. ed.; Valley Forge, Pennsylvania: Judson Press, 1969), 239.

[31] For a list of all of his works, see *Devoted to the Service of the Temple: Piety, Persecution, and Ministry in the Writings of Hercules Collins,* eds. Haykin and Weaver, 135-37.

[32] *History of the English Baptists*, III, 130.

[33] Piggott, *Mr. Hercules Collins*, 33-34.

Introduction | **19**

Calvinistic Baptist works in the city. As Piggott remarked to those who gathered for Collins' funeral on October 9: many of them were able to call Collins "father" for he had begotten them through the gospel.[34] Collins was ill only a few days before he died. So brief was the time of his illness that a good friend like Piggott was not able to find the time to visit him. According to some who were at Collins' bedside the day before he died, the Baptist pastor spoke with profound emotion of the implications of Revelation 12:11, "They overcame…by the blood of the Lamb."[35] He was buried in London's central burial ground for Baptists and Dissenters, Bunhill Fields.

The purpose of Collins' catechism

Hercules Collins seems to have had at least three purposes in publishing the OC. The catechism was to function as a tool for pastoral instruction, as a polemic against false teaching, and as a plea for doctrinal unity. Having become the pastor of the Wapping congregation only four years earlier, Collins modified the HC so as to use as a tool in fulfilling his pastoral duties. A comparison of the two documents reveals a number of edits, a good number of which are best explained as Collins' attempts to make the catechism more accessible to his local congregation. One example of this type of editing is found in Collins' rearrangement of the section dealing with the Ten Commandments. Whereas the HC listed the Ten Commandments all together then later explained them individually, Collins rearranged this section to allow for each

---

[34] Piggott, *Mr. Hercules Collins*, 34.
[35] Piggott, *Mr. Hercules Collins*, 35.

commandment to be listed separately along with its explanation and application. This rearrangement has an obvious pedagogical benefit. Collins explicitly stated this concern for the spiritual nurture of the local congregation to which he ministered in the following benediction that concluded his "Preface" to the catechism:

> And for those whom the Lord hath committed to my Charge, that the Eternal God may be your Refuge, and underneath you everlasting Arms; that Grace may be opened to your Hearts, and your hearts to Grace; that the blessing of the God of Abraham, Isaac and Jacob may be upon you, and the eternal Spirit may be with you, shall be the Prayer of your unworthy Brother, but more unworthy Pastor.

A second use of the OC was clearly stated by Collins on the title page: "Published For Preventing the Canker and Poison of Heresy and Error." This polemical focus of the catechism was necessary due to the fact that one of the leading church planters of the Calvinistic Baptist community in the early decades of their movement, Thomas Collier (d.1691),[36] had brought the Baptists into disrepute. In 1648, for example, Collier had denied the historic orthodox

---

[36] Thomas Collier was a native of Somerset and a key leader in the Western Association's adoption of the *Somerset Confession* in 1656. His career is riddled with doctrinal instability. For more information on the life and writings of Collier, see Richard Dale Land, "Doctrinal Controversies of English Particular Baptists (1644-1691) as Illustrated by the Career and Writings of Thomas Collier" (Unpublished D. Phil. Thesis, Regent's Park College, Oxford University, 1979).

understanding of the Trinity. Collier wrote that God

> is not, first, as some imagine, *Three Persons yet one God,* or three subsistings, distinguished though not divided; Its altogether impossible to distinguish God in this manner, and not divide him; thus to distinguish is to divide; for three persons are three not only distinguished, but divided: Some say there is, *God the Father, God the Son, and God the Holy Ghost, yet not three, but one God;* Let any one judge if here be not three Gods, if three then not one…[37]

In the words of Thomas Hall, an opponent of the Baptists, Collier was "a most dangerous and blasphemous Heretick [*sic*]," nothing less than an Arian, because he "denied the Trinity."[38] Although Hall was aware that Collier's beliefs were not shared by the generality of the Calvinistic Baptists,[39] others were not so discerning and took Collier's views as representative of the whole of his one-time co-religionists. Collins was concerned with defending his fellow Baptists against charges of heresy while at the same time providing an instrument of instruction in order to prevent the spread of further false teaching among their number.

A final reason that Collins published his OC was to identify himself and his fellow Particular Baptists as a part of the Reformed community throughout Europe. Collins thus

---

[37] *A General Epistle, To The Universal Church of the First Born: Whose Names are written in Heaven* (London: Giles Calvert, 1648), 4.

[38] *The Collier in his Colours: or, The Picture of a Collier* (London, 1652) in Hall's *The Font Guarded With XX Arguments* (London, 1652), 123, 125.

[39] *The Collier in his Colours* in *The Font Guarded*, 121, 125.

noted in his preface, "I concenter [sic] with the most orthodox divines in the fundamental principles and articles of the Christian Faith."[40] As Collins further wrote:

> albeit there are some differences between many godly divines and us in church constitution, yet inasmuch as those things are not the essence of Christianity, but that we do agree in the fundamental doctrine thereof, there is sufficient ground to lay aside all bitterness and prejudice, and labor to maintain a spirit of love each to other, knowing we shall never see all alike here.[41]

Both the choice of the HC as the basis for his catechism and the use of the word "orthodox" in the title highlight Collins' interest in identifying himself with historic Protestant orthodoxy. As James Renihan writes of Collins' choice of a title:

> While it obviously refers to the true character of the doctrines it promotes, it also identifies the source of those doctrines, the so-called Protestant Orthodox divines of Europe. Collins was making an emphatic statement: just as they are Orthodox, so also are we.[42]

---

[40] Collins, "Preface" to *Orthodox Catechism*, [iv]; Renihan, *True Confessions*, 237.

[41] Collins, "Preface" to *Orthodox Catechism*, [v]; Renihan, *True Confessions*, 237.

[42] Renihan, *True Confessions*, 235.

Similarities between the two catechisms

Further comparison of the OC and HC reveals that out of 129 questions in the HC (the original OC is not numbered), there are only eleven substantial changes: ten questions have been added to the OC and there has been one omitted. Collins faithfully followed the HC in beginning with the question that historian Philip Schaff has called "the whole gospel in a nutshell."[43]

> Quest. What is thy only comfort in life and death?
> Answ. That both in soul and body whether I live or die, I am not mine own, but belong wholly unto my faithful Lord and Savior Jesus Christ: who by his most precious blood, fully satisfying for all my sins, hath delivered me from all the power of the devil, and so preserveth me, that without the will of my heavenly Father, not so much as an hair may fall from my head; yea all things must serve for my safety: Wherefore by his Spirit also he assureth me of everlasting life, and maketh me ready and prepared, that henceforth I may live to him.[44]

The basic structure of the OC then follows the pattern of the HC such that all of the theological topics contained in the HC are also covered in OC.[45] Typical of the way that Collins

---

[43] *The Creeds of Christendom* (Grand Rapids: Baker Book House, 2007), I, 541.

[44] Collins, *Orthodox Catechism*, 1; Renihan, *True Confessions*, 239.

[45] Although the section on baptism in OC is dramatically altered, the topic was still covered. There are also questions added to certain topics by Collins.

24 | *An Orthodox Catechism*

sought to follow the HC closely was his treatment of the Apostles' Creed.

Both the HC and its Baptist counterpart are desirous of affirming core elements of the historic catholic teaching of the Ancient Church, of which the central one is the Trinity.[46] Thus, matching the HC word for word, the OC asks: "Into how many parts is this Creed divided?" The answer: "Into three: the first of the eternal Father, and our creation: the second, of the Son and our redemption: the third, of the Holy Ghost, and our sanctification."[47] In clear contrast to the heterodoxy expressed by Thomas Collier with regard to the Trinity, the OC then asserted the biblical doctrine in these words:

> Q. Seeing there is but one only substance of God, why namest thou those three, the Father, the Son, and the Holy Ghost?
> A. Because God hath so manifested himself in his Word, that these three distinct persons are that one true everlasting God.[48]

Although following the HC fully in its exposition of the Apostles' Creed, Collins did see fit to make a couple of minor, albeit not unimportant, changes. In the margin alongside the

---

[46] Collins' OC actually included the Nicene Creed of 325–interestingly enough, not the Niceno-Constantinopolitan Creed of 381–and the Athanasian Creed at the close of his catechism: Collins, *Orthodox Catechism*, 71-74; Renihan, *True Confessions*, 284-87.

[47] Collins, *Orthodox Catechism*, 9; Renihan, *True Confessions*, 244.

[48] Collins, *Orthodox Catechism*, 9; Renihan, *True Confessions*, 244. Collins has added an "and" between "true" and "everlasting."

text of the Apostles' Creed, Collins provided two caveats. On the phrase "He descended into Hell", Collins adds: "Not that he, (to wit, Christ) went into the place of the damned, but that he went absolutely into the state of the dead. See Dr. Usher [*sic*] of Christ, in his body of divinity, pag. 174. and Mr. Perkins on the Creed."[49] In this note, Collins referred first to the 1670 London edition of James Ussher's (1581–1656) well-known *A Body of Divinity*, which is structured like a catechism and where the Irish Puritan asked at one point, "What is meant by his [i.e. Christ's] descending into hell?" He answered, "Not that he went to the place of the damned, but that he went absolutely unto the estate of the dead."[50] In the next question, Ussher further explained what he understands by Christ's going to the "estate of the dead." It entails him going "in his soul into heaven" while he "was in his body under the very power and dominion of death for a season."[51] Usher thus gave Collins a way to understand this element of Christian theology. Puritan theologian William Perkins (1558–1602), on the other hand, in the work that Collins referred to, had doubts about the phrase "he descended into hell" being part of the original Apostles' Creed.[52] Nevertheless, he did provide four possible interpretations[53] and opted for the view that Christ's descent into hell was simply his being "held

---

[49] Collins, *Orthodox Catechism*, 8; Renihan, *True Confessions*, 244 and 290, n.xxxv.

[50] James Ussher, *A Body of Divinity: Or The Sum and Substance of Christian Religion* (London: Nath[aniel] Ranew and J[onathan] Robinson, 1670), 174.

[51] Ussher, *Body of Divinity*, 174.

[52] *An Exposition of the Symbole or Creede of the Apostles, according to the Tenour of the Scriptures, and the Consent of Orthodoxe Fathers of the Church* (London: John Legatt, 1631), 260-61.

[53] *Exposition of the Symbole or Creede*, 261-67.

captive in the grave" and lying "in bondage under death for the space of three days."[54] In other words, Perkins and Ussher were in essential agreement about the interpretation of this clause, an interpretation that Collins wished to endorse in view of any possible ambiguity on this issue in the HC.

Collins also added a marginal note alongside the statement, "I believe in…the holy catholic church": "Not that we are to believe in, but that there is a Catholic church, and by Catholic, we mean no more than the universal church, which is a company chosen out of whole mankind unto everlasting life, by the Word & Spirit of God."[55] In this sentence Collins merges two streams of seventeenth-century British ecclesial reflection: the commitment to catholicity, a fundamental mark of the church asserted by Ancient Christianity, as well as the upholding of the Congregationalist principle of the gathered church. In fact, this statement distinctly recalled a classic statement of Baptist ecclesiology in the First London Confession of Faith (1644/1646). There it was stated that Christ has "a spiritual Kingdom, which is the Church, which he hath purchased and redeemed to himself" and that this Church is visibly manifest in the local "company of visible Saints, called and separated from the world, by the word and Spirit of God."[56]

The sacraments in the catechisms
Whereas the Second London Confession of Faith (1677,

---

[54] *Exposition of the Symbole or Creede*, 265.

[55] Collins, *Orthodox Creed*, 8; Renihan, *True Confessions*, 244 and 290, n.xxxvii.

[56] First London Confession of Faith 33 in William L. Lumpkin, *Baptist Confessions of Faith* (Valley Forge, Pennsylvania: Judson Press, 1969), 165.

1689)[57] changes the term "sacrament" in the Westminster Confession of Faith (1646) to "ordinance", no such alteration is present in the OC. Given the predilection of later Baptists for the term "ordinance" when speaking about baptism and the Lord's Supper, and their disagreement with the Reformed consensus about the subjects of baptism, Collins' treatment of the sacraments is also noteworthy in what he did and did not change from the HC. Although Collins was not hesitant to alter this catechism where he believed it to be warranted by Scripture, he obviously had no problem using the word "sacrament" and retaining the definition used in the HC[58]-language that can be traced back to authors such as Philip Melanchthon (1497–1560), John Calvin (1509–1564), and Heinrich Bullinger (1504–1575).[59] For example, delineating the

---

[57] Second London Confession of Faith 28-30 in Lumpkin, *Baptist Confessions of Faith*,

[58] Stanley K. Fowler argues in his *More Than A Symbol: The British Baptist Recovery of Baptismal Sacramentalism* (London: Paternoster Press, 2002) that the changing of the terminology from "sacrament" to "ordinance" in the Second London Confession of Faith (1677/1688) does not mean that Baptists had embraced a non-sacramental view of baptism. Among the reasons that he cites for this conclusion are: "the terms 'sacrament' and 'ordinance' were often used synonymously by Baptists of that era, including signatories of this confession" and "Chapter XXX of the Second London Confession interpreted the Lord's Supper in the Westminister tradition along the lines of a 'spiritual presence' of Christ which is mediated through the Supper, i.e., the Calvinistic as opposed to the Zwinglian view." (*More Than A Symbol*, 17).

[59] There is no scholarly consensus as to whether the HC is primarily indebted to Huldreich Zwingli (1484–1531), Melanchthon, or Calvin in its description of the sacraments. Lyle D. Bierma has argued persuasively in his monograph *The Doctrine of the Sacraments in the Heidelberg Catechism: Melanchthonian, Calvinist, or Zwinglian?* (Studies in Reformed Theology and History, n.s., no. 4; Princeton: Princeton Theological Seminary, 1999) that the language of the HC on the sacraments is intentionally vague on matters on

source that issues in the faith that alone makes us "partakers of Christ and his benefits," the OC stated: it is from "the Holy Ghost, who kindleth it in our hearts by the preaching of the Gospel, and other Ordinances, and confirmeth it by the use of the Sacraments."[60] Following the lead of the HC, the OC then proceeded to limit the sacraments to baptism and the Lord's Supper, which are defined as the "sacred Signes [sic], and Seals, set before our Eyes, and ordained of God for this cause, that he may declare and seal by them the Promise of his Gospel unto us."[61] Thus, the sacraments function to assure us "that the Salvation of all of us standeth in the only Sacrifice of Christ, offered for us upon the Cross."[62]

The extent of Collins' commitment to the use of the term "sacrament" is revealed by his use of the phrase "other ordinances" in his rendition of the answer to HC's question 65. Collins seems to have made a clear distinction between "ordinances" and the "sacraments." The former included preaching,[63] prayer,[64] the laying-on-of-hands,[65] as well as

---

which the major leaders of the Reformation would disagree. This language has been chosen specifically to accommodate all the viewpoints of the Reformation (with the exception of the pre-Melanchtonian unmodified Lutheran view). For the purpose of this essay, it is sufficient to note that the language on the sacraments is grounded in a Reformation understanding, albeit as a consensus statement.

[60] Collins, *Orthodox Catechism*, 25; Renihan, *True Confessions*, 254. In Renihan's parallel version of the HC and OC at this point, he renders them identical. In actuality, Collins has added the phrase "and other Ordinances." For discussion, see below.

[61] Collins, *Orthodox Catechism*, 25; Renihan, *True Confessions*, 254.

[62] Collins, *Orthodox Catechism*, 26; Renihan, *True Confessions*, 254.

[63] Collins, *Orthodox Catechism*, 25.

hymn-singing[66]–and Collins could even describe baptism[67] and the Lord's Supper as such.[68] But, in accord with the Protestant tradition that was evident in the HC, Collins restricted the sacraments to baptism and the Lord's Supper. As much as he could, Collins wished to be found in accord with other Protestant divines. And this desire is especially seen in Collins' eucharistic theology.

Some modern-day Baptist theologians[69] might be surprised to learn that there is virtually no change between a sixteenth-century Reformed document and a seventeenth-century Baptist document on the issue of the Lord's Supper. But that is exactly what one finds when the sections about the Lord's Table in the HC and OC are examined side by side. For example, the HC stated that when a believer partakes of the Lord's Supper, he or she may say: "my soul is no less assuredly fed to everlasting life with his body, which was crucified for us, and his blood, which was shed for us; than I

---

[64] See Collins, *Orthodox Catechism*, 37; Renihan, *True Confessions*, 262, where Collins includes prayer with baptism and preaching, both of which he regards as ordinances.

[65] Collins, *Orthodox Catechism*, 33-34; Renihan, *True Confessions*, 260.

[66] "An Appendix concerning the Ordinance of Singing" in Collins, *Orthodox Catechism*, 75-86.

[67] *Believers-Baptism from Heaven, and of Divine Institution. Infants-Baptism from Earth, and Human Invention* (London, 1691), 15, 17; *The Antidote proved A Counterfeit: or, Error detected, and Believers Baptism Vindicated* (London: William Marshall, 1693), 8.

[68] Collins, *Orthodox Catechism*, 33-34; Renihan, *True Confessions*, 266

[69] For example, Thomas White, after explaining Calvin's view of the spiritual presence of Christ in the Lord's Supper, dismissively writes, "This view has not found favor among Baptists" ["A Baptist's Theology of the Lord's Supper" in his, Jason G. Duesing, and Malcolm B. Yarnell, III, eds., *Restoring Integrity in Baptist Churches* (Grand Rapids: Kregel, 2008), 148].

receive and taste by the mouth of my body the bread and wine, the signs of the body and blood of our Lord, received at the hand of the minister."[70] Collins' OC made but one change to this. In the place of "us" was "me," driving home the experiential nature of the Supper.

Further, "to eat the body of Christ" at the Lord's Table not only involves embracing with an "assured confidence of mind" that "forgiveness of sins and everlasting life" come through "the whole passion and death of Christ," but it also entails being "more and more…united to his sacred body, that though he be in heaven, and we on earth, yet nevertheless are we flesh of his flesh, and bone of his bones." And this union between Christ and his people happens through the work of "the Holy Ghost, who dwelleth both in Christ and us."[71] From Collins' perspective, although the risen Christ's body is in heaven, his people have communion with him in the Supper through the Spirit.[72]

Major changes and additions

The most noticeable change made by Collins in the OC is the change of the section dealing with baptism. Collins' desire to promote unity between Baptists and other Protestant groups did not cause him to compromise this Baptist distinctive. In fact, in his preface which calls for unity on the "essence of Christianity," Collins stated that he only differed with the

---

[70] Collins, *Orthodox Catechism*, 39; Renihan, *True Confessions*, 263.

[71] Collins, *Orthodox Catechism*, 39; Renihan, *True Confessions*, 263-64.

[72] See further Michael A. G. Haykin, " 'His soul-refreshing presence': The Lord's Supper in Calvinistic Baptist Thought and Experience in the 'Long' Eighteenth Century" in Anthony R. Cross and Philip E. Thompson, eds., *Baptist Sacramentalism* (London: Paternoster Press, 2003), 181.

"orthodox divines" in "some things about Church-constitution, wherein I have taken a little pains to show you the true form of God's house."[73] The first hint within the catechism that Collins would make a significant change on the subject of baptism is found when he inserts the phrase "figured out in holy Baptism" into the answer to question 43 of the HC.[74] This answer describes the believer's sharing with Christ in his crucifixion, death, and burial. Collins' insertion of the phrase about baptism demonstrates the importance of the symbol's correspondence to the thing signified for seventeenth-century Baptists.

Although the questions describing the meaning of baptism remain unchanged in the OC, Collins has added a complete section on the mode and proper subjects of baptism. This illustrates that the Baptist quarrel with their Reformed brothers and sisters was not so much over the understanding of the meaning of baptism (at least as it applied to adults). Their disagreement was over the mode of baptism and the identity of the sacrament's appropriate recipients. In answer to the question "What is Baptism?"–which is conspicuous by its absence in the HC–Collins essentially reproduced the description of baptism from the Second London Confession of Faith, which had first appeared three year earlier in 1677: "Immersion or dipping of the person in water in the name of the Father, Son, and Holy Ghost, by such who are duly qualified by Christ."[75] Having answered the question of

---

[73] Collins, "Preface" to *Orthodox Catechism*, [iv]; Renihan, *True Confessions*, 237.

[74] Collins, *Orthodox Catechism*, 16; Renihan, *True Confessions*, 248.

[75] Collins, *Orthodox Catechism*, 26; Renihan, *True Confessions*, 255. Cf. the Second London Confession of Faith 29.3-4. There is nothing in the Second

32 | *An Orthodox Catechism*

mode with this definition, this answer begged the question: "Who are the proper subjects of this ordinance?" The response came almost word for word from the Second London Confession: "Those who do actually profess repentance towards God, faith in, and obedience to our Lord Jesus Christ."[76] The only difference between the OC and the Second London Confession is that the OC has the word "Christ." Collins continued his treatment of baptism by denying the validity of the baptism of infants based upon the fact that Scripture nowhere commands it.[77] This is followed by a series of questions providing an extensive rebuttal of arguments for infant baptism from covenant theology.[78] From this point on, Collins resumed following the HC in its treatment of the meaning of baptism. The discussion of the mode and proper recipients of baptism thus constitutes the main area of divergence between the two catechisms.

There are four further notable additions to the HC in the OC. For the most part, these do not reflect a disagreement with the framers of the HC, but a special emphasis that Collins wished to add in his edition. To the section on baptism is added a series of questions and answers regarding the laying-on-of-hands upon the baptized. To the section on the Lord's Supper is added a question regarding the singing of a hymn after the Supper. Between the Lord's Prayer and its exposition is added a question on whether Christians are tied

---

London Confession about a properly qualified administrator. This clause in Collins' OC speaks of his high view of an ordained ministry.

[76] Collins, *Orthodox Catechism*, 26; Renihan, *True Confessions*, 255. See the Second London Confession of Faith 29.2.

[77] Collins, *Orthodox Catechism*, 26-27; Renihan, *True Confessions*, 255.

[78] Collins, *Orthodox Catechism*, 27-31; Renihan, *True Confessions*, 255-58.

to written prayers. Finally, at the very end of the catechism there have been added the Nicene and Athanasian Creeds. Why did Collins introduce these additions?

First, with regard to the laying-on-of-hands and hymn-singing, Collins believed both of these to be vital ordinances of God for the spiritual health of the Church. In his insistence that the laying-on-of-hands upon the baptized was commanded by Scripture, Collins represents a minority position among seventeenth-century Particular Baptists, although this was a commonly-held belief among the General Baptists of the period.[79] The other notable representative of this view among the Particular Baptists was Collins' fellow London Baptist, Benjamin Keach (1640–1704), who defended this conviction in *Darkness Vanquished: or, Truth in it's Primitive purity* (1675), later published in a second edition twenty-three years as *Laying on of Hands upon Baptized Believers, As such, Proved an Ordinance of Christ*. For both Keach and Collins, "the ordinance has a deeply experimental significance" and speaks primarily of assurance of salvation.[80] As Collins put it:

---

[79] See, for example, the Orthodox Creed 32 (1678) in Lumpkin, *Baptist Confessions of Faith*, 320-21.

[80] J. K. Parratt, "An Early Baptist on the Laying on of Hands", *The Baptist Quarterly*, 21 (1966), 325-27, 320. See also the discussion by Austin Walker, *The Excellent Benjamin Keach* (Dundas, Ontario: Joshua Press, 2004), 186-88. In some ways, this conviction is a variant of the belief held by some Puritans about the sealing of the Spirit. See, with regard to the latter, Adam Embry, " 'Keeper of the Great Seal of Heaven': Sealing of the Spirit in the Thought of John Flavel" (Th.M. thesis, The Southern Baptist Theological Seminary, 2008) and Choon-Gill Chae, "Thomas Goodwin's Doctrine of the Sealing of the Holy Spirit" (Th.M. thesis, Toronto Baptist Seminary and Bible College, 2010).

> Christ's ministers laying their hands solemnly upon the head of the baptized, with prayer to Almighty God for an increase of the graces and gifts of the Holy Ghost,...enable us to hold fast the faith which we now visibly own, having entered into the church by holy Baptism, and also be helped thereby to maintain constant war against the world, flesh and Devil.[81]

With regard to hymn-singing as an ordinance, this was a matter of no small controversy among the Baptists in the two decades following the publication of Collins' OC, especially during the 1690s.[82] Collins actually included a substantial appendix to the catechism that was devoted to this subject. In the catechism itself, he simply asked and answered the question, "How ought this ordinance of the Lord's Supper be closed?" *In nuce*, Collins' answer was: with "singing praises to God." Singing is the fit response to God "for his great benefits and blessings" given to the Church of Christ in the death of the Lord Jesus. Moreover, if the Lord and his apostolic band finished the last supper with a hymn and "if Christ did sing, who was going to die, what cause have we to sing for whom he died, that we might not eternally die, but live a spiritual

---

[81] Collins, *Orthodox Catechism*, 34; Renihan, *True Confessions*, 260.

[82] On the hymn-singing controversy, see Murdina D. MacDonald, "London Calvinistic Baptists, 1689–1727: Tensions Within a Dissenting Community Under Toleration" (D.Phil. thesis, Regent's Park College, University of Oxford, 1982), 49-82; Walker, *Excellent Benjamin Keach*, 275-303; Michael A.G. Haykin and C. Jeffrey Robinson, "Particular Baptist Debates about Communion and Hymn-Singing" in Michael A.G. Haykin and Mark Jones, eds., *'Drawn into Controversie': Reformed Theological Diversity and Debates Within Seventeenth-Century British Puritanism* (Göttingen: Vandenhoeck & Ruprecht, 2011), 293-305.

and eternal life with Father, Son, and Spirit in unexpressible glory."[83]

A third significant change has to do with the Lord's Prayer. Following the HC discussion of why believers need to pray and that catechism's introduction to the Lord's Prayer, Collins inserted a question into the OC that asks whether or not Christians must use the very form of this prayer in worship.[84] This was a very important issue since the ejection of the Puritans from their churches in 1662 was bound up with their refusal to lead worship according to the exact words of the Book of Common Prayer. More generally, there had been disputes within the Puritan movement about the propriety of using written prayers at all.[85] Collins asserted that the form of the Lord's Prayer is "nothing else but a set or course of certain heads or generals, whereunto all benefits both corporal and spiritual may be referred" and thus concluded that "the form of a prayer delivered unto us by

---

[83] Collins, *Orthodox Catechism*, 44-45; Renihan, *True Confessions*, 266-67. Renihan has "inexpressible glory."

[84] Collins, *Orthodox Catechism*, 65-66; Renihan, *True Confessions*, 281-82.

[85] For this debate about prayer, see especially Geoffrey F. Nuttall, *The Holy Spirit in Puritan Faith and Experience* (2nd ed.; Oxford: Basil Blackwell, 1947), 62-74; A. G. Matthews, "The Puritans at Prayer" in his *Mr. Pepys and Nonconformity* (London: Independent Press, 1954), 100-22; Garth B. Wilson, "The Puritan Doctrine of the Holy Spirit: A Critical Investigation of a Crucial Chapter in the History of Protestant Theology" (Th.D. Dissertation, Knox College, Toronto, 1978), 208-23; Alan L. Hayes, "Spirit and Structure in Elizabethan Public Prayer" in E. J. Furcha, ed., *Spirit Within Structure: Essays in Honor of George Johnston on the Occasion of His Seventieth Birthday* (Allison Park, PA: Pickwick Publications, 1983), 117-32; Horton Davies, *The Worship of the English Puritans* (1948 ed.; repr. Morgan, PA: Soli Deo Gloria, 1997), 98-161.

36 | *An Orthodox Catechism*

Christ is wholly a thing indifferent."[86] Finally, at the very close of the OC, Collins added in full two more classical creedal statements from the Ancient Church, the Nicene and Athanasian Creeds, clear indications of Collins' desire to affirm continuity with the best of the Ancient Church and classical orthodoxy.[87]

The regulative principle as the explanation for the Orthodox Catechism's edits

Having detailed the way in which Hercules Collins edited the contents of the HC for his catechism, an assessment as to the basis upon which he edited the HC is now appropriate. In all of the decisions that Collins made regarding the content of his catechism, there is one recurring theme: the authority of Scripture to govern our thought, worship, and life. This principle is stated succinctly in the OC in answer to the question of what the second commandment requires. The answer: "That we should not express or represent God by any image or shape and figure, or worship him any otherwise than he hath commanded himself in his Word to be worshiped."[88] This is nothing other than the Reformed regulative principle *in nuce*.[89] For example, though desirous to

---

[86] Collins, *Orthodox Catechism*, 65-66; Renihan, *True Confessions*, 281-82.

[87] Collins, *Orthodox Catechism,* 71-74; Renihan, *True Confessions*, 284-87. See also Collins' explicit remarks about these creeds in his "Preface": Collins, *Orthodox Catechism*, [vi-vii]; Renihan, *True Confessions*, 238.

[88] Collins, *Orthodox Catechism,* 52; Renihan, *True Confessions*, 272-73.

[89] For a classic Puritan treatment of the regulative principle, see Jeremiah Burroughs, *Gospel Worship* (repr. Morgan, PA: Soli Deo Gloria Publications, 1990). Interestingly, the early English Baptist historian Thomas Crosby uses Burroughs' (a paedobaptist) own words to argue for Baptist principles in the Preface to his *The History of the English Baptists* (London, 1738), I, xi–xiii.

show his unity with other orthodox Protestant divines outside of his own ecclesial community, Collins nevertheless rejected their understanding of baptism. He denied the validity of infant baptism with this lapidary remark: "We have neither precept nor example for that practice in all the Book of God."[90] And to the question, "Doth the Scripture any where expressly forbid the baptizing of infants?," Collins replied:

> It is sufficient that the Divine Oracle commands the baptizing of believers, unless we will make ourselves wiser than what is written. Nadab and Abihu were not forbidden to offer strange fire, yet for so doing they incurred God's wrath, because they were commanded to take fire from the altar.[91]

For Collins, it was the Reformation's regulative principle of worship that required the rejection of infant baptism. This was also his argument in his major treatise on baptism entitled *Believers-Baptism from Heaven, and of Divine Institution*. There Collins wrote that his intention in publishing this book was

> to display this Sacrament in its apostolic primitive purity, free from the adulterations of men, a sin which God charged upon the learned Jews, that they made void the commands of God by their traditions. O that none of the learned among the Gentiles,

---

[90] Collins, *Orthodox Catechism*, 26-27; Renihan, *True Confessions*, 255.
[91] Collins, *Orthodox Catechism*, 26-27; Renihan, *True Confessions*, 255.

especially those of the Reformed churches, may be charged with setting up men's inventions in the room of Christ's institutions.[92]

This helps explain why Collins would retain so much of a Reformed document, while rejecting its teaching on infant baptism. He believed that the catechism's teaching elsewhere was justified by Scripture, but where it was not, Collins was bound to follow Scripture.

Collins' commitment to the regulative principle is perhaps most clearly seen in the "Preface" to his catechism where, in the midst of an appeal for Christian unity based on a common commitment to the "fundamental principles and articles of the Christian faith," he explained his "differing in some things about Church-constitution." He expressed his hope that his zeal for "the true form of God's house" will not be misunderstood. As he explained:

> That God whom we serve is very jealous of his worship; and forasmuch as by his providence the law of his house hath been preserved and continued to us, we look upon it as our duty in our generation to be searching out the mind of God in his holy oracle, as Ezra and Nehemiah did the Feast of Tabernacles, and to reform what is amiss; As Hezekiah, who took a great deal of pains to cleanse the House of God, and set all things in order, that were out of order, particularly caused the people to keep the Passover according to the Institution: for it had not, saith the

---

[92] *Believers-Baptism from Heaven, and of Divine Institution*, 7.

text, been of a long time kept in such sort as it was written; and albeit the pure institutions of Christ were not for some hundreds of years practiced according to the due order, or very little, through the innovations of antichrist; and as circumcision for about forty years was unpracticed in the wilderness, yet as Joshua puts this duty in practice as soon as God signified his mind in that particular, so we having our judgments informed about the true way of worship, do not dare to stifle the light God hath given us.[93]

Though the baptism of believers may have been largely lost for centuries, it had now been recovered as a direct result of a renewed emphasis on the authority and sufficiency of the Word of God in the Protestant Reformation. Collins' zeal for worship regulated by God's Word drove him to reject the human innovation of infant baptism. In so doing, he was never more true to the spirit of orthodox Protestantism even as his OC stands as a witness to his deep desire to truly "concenter with the most orthodox divines."

---

[93] Collins, "Preface" to *Orthodox Catechism*, [iv–v]; Renihan, *True Confessions*, 237.

Chapter 1

General Introduction and The First Part: Of Man's Misery

A Catechism containing the Sum of Christian Religion

Q. 1. What is your only comfort in life and death?

A. That both in soul and body (a), whether I live or die (b), I am not my own, but belong wholly unto my most faithful Lord and Savior Jesus Christ (c). By His most precious blood fully satisfying for all my sins (d), He has delivered me from all the power of the devil (e), and so preserves me (f), that without the will of my heavenly Father not so much as a hair may fall from my head (g). Yes, all things must serve for my safety (h) and by His Spirit, also He assures me of everlasting life (i), and makes me ready and prepared (j), that from now on I may live to Him.
(a) 1 Cor. 6:19; 1 Thess. 5:10.
(b) Rom. 14:8.

(c) 1 Cor. 3:23.
(d) 1 Pet. 1:18-19; 1 John 1:7; 2:2.
(e) 1 John 3:8; Heb. 2:14-15.
(f) John 6:39.
(g) Matt. 10:30; Luke 21:18.
(h) Rom. 8:28.
(i) 2 Cor. 1:12; 5:5; Eph. 1:13-14.
(j) Rom. 8:24-25.

Q. 2. How many things are necessary for you to know that, enjoying this comfort, you may live and die happily?

A. Three. The first, what is the greatness of my sin and misery (a). The second, how I am delivered from all sin and misery (b). The third, what thanks I owe to God for this delivery (c).
(a) Luke 24:47; Rom. 3:23.
(b) Rom. 8:15; 1 Cor. 6:11; Titus 3:3-8.
(c) Matt. 5:16; Rom. 6:11-13; Eph. 5:10; Titus 2:11-12; 1 Pet. 2:9; 3:10-12.

THE FIRST PART
Of Man's Misery

Q. 3. From what source do you know your misery?

A. From the law of God (a).

(a) Rom. 3:20; 5:20; 7:5, 13.

Q. 4. What does the law of God require of us?

A. That which Christ summarily teaches us, Matthew 22:37-40. You shall love the Lord your God with all your heart, with all your soul, and with all your mind, and with all your strength (a). This is the first and the great commandment; and the second is like it, You shall love your neighbor as yourself. On these two commandments hang the whole Law and the Prophets.
(a) Luke 10:27.

Q. 5. Are you able to keep all these things perfectly?

A. No (a). By nature I am prone to the hatred of God and of my neighbors (b).
(a) Rom. 3:10, 23; 1 John 1:8.
(b) Rom. 8:7; Eph. 2:3; Titus 3:3.

Q. 6. Did God then make man so wicked and perverse?

A. Not so (a). He made him good, and in His own image (b), endowing him with true righteousness and holiness (c), that he might rightly know God his Creator, and heartily love Him, and live with Him blessed forever, and that to laud and magnify Him (d).

General Introduction and The First Part: Of Man's Misery

(a) Gen. 1:31.
(b) Gen. 1:26-27.
(c) Eph. 4:24; Col. 3:10.
(d) 2 Cor. 3:18.

Q. 7. From what source does the wickedness of man's nature arise?

A. From the fall and disobedience of our first parents, Adam and Eve (a). For this reason our nature is so corrupt and we are all conceived and born in sin (b).
(a) Rom. 5:12, 18-19.
(b) Gen. 5:3; Psa. 51:5.

Q. 8. Are we so corrupt that we are not at all able to do well and are prone to all vice?

A. Indeed we are, except we are regenerated by the Holy Spirit (a).
(a) Gen. 6:5; Job 14:4; 15:16; Isa. 53:6; John 3:5.

Q. 9. Does not God, then, do injury to man who in the law requires that of him which he is not able to perform?

A. No. God made man such a one as he might perform it (a), but man, by the impulsion of the devil (b) and his own stubbornness bereaved himself and all his posterity of those divine graces (c).

(a) Eccl. 7:29.
(b) Gen. 3.
(c) Rom. 5:12-21.

Q. 10. Does God leave this stubbornness and falling away of man unpunished?

A. No. He is angry in a most dreadful manner (a), for the sins wherein we are born and which we ourselves commit. In a most just judgment, He punishes them with present and everlasting punishments as He pronounces: "Cursed is he that does not confirm all the words of this law to do them" (b).

(a) Rom. 5:12.
(b) Deut. 27:26; Gal. 3:10.

Q. 11. Is not God therefore merciful?

A. Yes, very much so! He is merciful (a), but He is also just (b), wherefore His justice requires that the same which is committed against the divine majesty of God should also be recompensed with extreme, that is, everlasting punishment both in body and soul.

(a) Exod. 34:6; Psa. 5:4-6.
(b) Exod. 20:5.

General Introduction and The First Part: Of Man's Misery

Chapter 2

The Second Part:
Of Man's Redemption
(Introductory Questions)

THE SECOND PART
Of Man's Redemption

Q. 12. Seeing, then, by the just judgment of God we are subject both to temporal and eternal punishments, is there yet any way or means remaining whereby we may be delivered from these punishments and be reconciled to God?

A. God will have His justice satisfied (a). Therefore, it is necessary that we satisfy it either by ourselves or by another (b).
(a) Exod. 20:5, 7; 23:7.
(b) Rom. 8:3.

Q. 13. Are we able to satisfy God's justice by ourselves?

A. Not one bit. Instead, we increase our debt every day (a).
(a) Job 9:2-3; 15:15; Matt. 6:12.

Q. 14. Is there any creature in heaven or in earth, which is only a creature, able to satisfy for us?

A. None. For first, God will not punish that sin which man has committed in any other creature; and second, neither can that which is nothing but a creature sustain the wrath of God against sin and deliver others from it (a).
(a) Job 4:18; 25:5; Psa. 130:3; Heb. 2:14-18; 10:5-10.

Q. 15. What manner of mediator and deliverer, then, must we seek for?

A. Such a one as is very man and perfectly just, and yet in power above all creatures, that is, one who also is very (f) God (a).
(a) Isa. 7:14; 53:11; Jer. 23:6; Rom. 8:3; 1 Cor. 15:25; 2 Cor. 5:14; Heb. 7:16.

Q. 16. Why is it necessary that the mediator be very man and perfectly just as well?

A. Because the justice of God requires that the same human nature which has sinned do itself likewise make recompense for sin (a); but he that is himself a sinner, cannot make recompense for others (b).

(a) Rom. 5:12, 17.
(b) 1 Pet. 3:18; Heb. 7:26.

Q. 17. Why must he also be very God?

A. That He might by the power of His Godhead sustain in His flesh the burden of God's wrath (a) and might recover and restore to us that righteousness and life which we lost (b).
(a) Isa. 55:3, 8; Acts 2:24; 1 Pet. 3:18.
(b) John 3:16; Acts 20:28; 1 John 1:2; 4:9-10.

Q. 18. And who is that mediator which is together both very God and very perfectly a just man?

A. Even our Lord Jesus Christ (a) who is made to us of God's wisdom, righteousness, sanctification and redemption (b).
(a) Matt. 1:23; Luke 2:11; John 14:16; 1 Tim. 2:5; 3:16.
(b) 1 Cor. 1:30.

Q. 19. From what source do you know this?

A. Out of the gospel which God first made known in paradise (a), and afterwards did spread it abroad by the patriarchs and prophets (b), shadowed it by sacrifices and other ceremonies of the law (c), and lastly accomplished it by His only begotten Son, Christ our Lord (d).
(a) Gen. 3:15.
(b) Gen. 22:18; 49:10-11; Acts 3:22; 10:43; Rom. 1:2; Heb. 1:1.

The Second Part: Of Man's Redemption (Intro. Questions)

(c) John 5:46; Heb. 10:7ff.
(d) Rom. 10:4; Gal. 3:24; 4:4; Heb. 13:8.

Q. 20. Is, then, salvation restored by Christ to all men who perished in Adam?

A. Not at all, but to those only who by a true faith are ingrafted into or united with Him (a).
(a) Psa. 2:12; Isa. 53:11; John 1:12; 3:36; Rom. 11:20; Heb. 4:2; 10:39.

Q. 21. What is faith?

A. It is not only a knowledge, whereby I surely assent to all things which God has revealed to us in His Word (a), but also an assured trust (b) kindled in my heart by the Holy Spirit (c), through the gospel (d), whereby I make my repose in God being assuredly resolved that remission of sins, everlasting righteousness, and life is given not to others only, but to me also and that freely through the mercy of God for the merits of Christ alone (e).
(a) Heb. 11:1-3; Gal. 2:20; James 2:19.
(b) Rom. 4:16; 5:1; 10:10.
(c) Matt. 16:17; John 3:5; Acts 10:45; Gal. 5:22; Phil. 1:19.
(d) Mark 16:16; Acts 16:14; Rom. 1:16; 10:17; 1 Cor. 1:21.
(e) Acts 10:42-43; Rom. 3:24-25.

Q. 22. What are those things which are necessary for a

Christian man to believe?

A. All things which are promised us in the gospel. The sum of this is briefly comprised in the articles of the catholic and undoubted faith of all true Christians, commonly called the Apostles' Creed.

I believe in God the Father Almighty, Maker of heaven and earth, and in Jesus Christ His only Son, our Lord, who was conceived by the Holy Spirit, born of the virgin Mary, suffered under Pontius Pilate, was crucified, dead and buried, He descended into *hell, the third day He rose from the dead, and ascended into heaven, from where He shall come to judge both the living and the dead. I believe in the Holy Spirit, the holy +catholic Church, the communion of saints, the forgiveness of sins, the resurrection of the body, and the life everlasting. Amen.

*Not that He, (that is, Christ), went into the place of the damned, but that He went absolutely into the state of the dead. See Dr. Usher of Christ, in his *Body of Divinity*, page 174. and Mr. Perkins on the Creed.

+Not that we are to believe in, but that there is a catholic Church, and by catholic, we mean no more than the universal Church, which is a company chosen out of the whole of mankind to everlasting life, by the Word and Spirit of God.

Q. 23. Into how many parts is this Creed divided?

A. Into three: the first of the eternal Father, and our creation; the second of the Son, and our redemption; and the third of the Holy Spirit, and our sanctification.

Q. 24. Seeing there is but one only substance of God (a), why do you name those three, the Father, the Son, and the Holy Spirit?

A. Because God has manifested Himself in His Word that these three distinct persons are that one true everlasting God (b).

(a) Deut. 6:4; Isa. 44:6; 1 Cor. 8:4; Eph. 4:6.

(b) Psa. 110:1; Isa. 61:1; Matt. 3:16-17; 28:19; Luke 4:18; John 14:26; 15:26; 2 Cor. 13:14; Gal. 4:6; Eph. 2:18; Titus 3:5-6; 1 John 5:7.

Chapter 3

The Second Part: Of Man's Redemption (God the Father)

God the Father

Q. 25. What do you believe when you say, "I believe in God the Father Almighty, Maker of heaven and earth?"

A. I believe in the everlasting Father of our Lord Jesus Christ, who made of nothing heaven and earth (a), with all that are in them, who likewise upholds and governs the same by His eternal counsel (b) and providence. This God I believe to be my God and Father for Christ's sake (c), and therefore to trust in Him, and rely on Him (d), that I do not doubt that He will provide all things necessary both for my soul and body (e). But also, whatever evils He sends on me in this troublesome life, He will turn out to my safety (f), because both He is able to do it, being God Almighty, and willing to do it, being a bountiful Father (g).

(a) Gen. 1:1-2; Job 33:4; Psa. 33:6; Isa. 45:7; Acts 4:24; 14:15.

(b) Psa. 104:3; 115:3; Matt. 10:29; Rom. 11:36; Heb. 1:3.
(c) John 1:12; Rom. 8:15; Gal. 4:5-6; Eph. 1:5.
(d) Psa. 55:23.
(e) Matt. 6:26; Luke 12:22.
(f) Rom. 8:28.
(g) Isa. 46:4; Rom. 8:38-39; 10:12.

Q. 26. What is the providence of God?

A. The almighty power of God, everywhere present (a), whereby He does, as it were, by His hand uphold and govern heaven and earth (b), with all creatures therein, so that those things which grow in the earth, as likewise rain and drought, fruitfulness and barrenness, meat and drink, health and sickness, riches and poverty, in a word, all things come not rashly and by chance, but by His fatherly counsel and will (c).

(a) Psa. 94:9; Isa. 29:15; Ezek. 8:12; Acts 17:25.
(b) Heb. 1:2-3.
(c) Prov. 22:2; Jer. 5:24; John 9:3; Acts 14:17.

Q. 27. What does this knowledge of the creation and providence of God profit us?

A. That in adversity we may be patient (a), and thankful in prosperity (b), and have hereafter our chief hope (c) reposed in God our most faithful Father. We can be sure that there is nothing which may withdraw us from His love (d), forasmuch as all creatures are so in His power, that without

His will they are not able not only to do anything, but not so much as once to move (e).
(a) Job 1:21; Rom. 5:3.
(b) Deut. 8:10; 1 Thess. 5:18.
(c) Rom. 5:4-5.
(d) Rom. 8:19, 38.
(e) Job 1:12; 2:6; Prov. 21:1; Acts 17:27.

The Second Part: Of Man's Redemption (God the Father)

Chapter 4

The Second Part: Of Man's Redemption (God the Son)

God the Son

Q. 28. Why is the Son of God called Jesus, that is, a Savior?

A. Because He saves us from our sins (a); neither ought any safety to be sought from any other (b), nor can it be found elsewhere.
(a) Matt. 1:21.
(b) Acts 4:12; Heb. 7:25.

Q. 29. Do they then who seek for happiness and safety of the saints, or of themselves, or elsewhere believe in the only Savior Jesus?

A. No. For although in word they boast themselves of Him as their only Savior, yet indeed they deny the only Savior Jesus

(a). For either Jesus is not a perfect Savior, or that those who embrace Him as their Savior with a true faith, possess all things in Him (b) which are required unto salvation.
(a) 1 Cor. 1:13, 30.
(b) Isa. 9:6; 43:11, 25; John 1:16; Col. 1:19-20; 2:10; Heb. 12:2.

Q. 30. Why is He called Christ, that is, Anointed?

A. Because He was ordained of the Father and anointed of the Holy Spirit (a) the chief Prophet and Teacher (b), who has opened unto us the secret counsel and all the will of His Father concerning our redemption (c). He was ordained and anointed the high Priest (d), who with that one only sacrifice of His body has redeemed us (e) and continually makes intercession to His Father for us (f). He was also ordained and anointed a King (g), who rules us by His Word and Spirit, and defends and maintains that salvation which He has purchased for us (h).
(a) Psa. 45:7; Heb. 1:9.
(b) Deut. 18:15; Acts 3:22.
(c) Matt. 11:27; John 1:18; 15:15.
(d) Heb. 7:21.
(e) Rom. 3:24; 5:9-10; Heb. 10:12.
(f) Heb. 7:25.
(g) Psa. 2:6; Luke 1:33.
(h) Matt. 28:18.

Q. 31. But why are you called a Christian?

A. Because through faith I am a member of Jesus Christ (a), and partaker of His anointing (b), that both I may confess His name (c), and present myself unto Him a living sacrifice of thankfulness (d), and also may in this life fight against sin and Satan with a free and good conscience (e), and afterwards enjoy an everlasting kingdom with Christ (f).
(a) Acts 11:26; 1 Cor. 6:15.
(b) 1 John 2:27.
(c) Matt. 10:32.
(d) Rom. 12:1; Heb. 13:15; 1 Pet. 2:5; Rev. 5:8.
(e) Rom. 6:12-13; 1 Tim. 1:18-19.
(f) 2 Tim. 2:12; Rev. 1:6.

Q. 32. For what cause is Christ called the only begotten Son of God, when we also are the sons of God?

A. Because Christ alone is the eternal and natural Son of the eternal Father (a), and we are but sons adopted of the Father by grace for His sake (b).
(a) John 3:16; Rom. 8:3; Heb. 1:2-3.
(b) John 1:12; Gal. 4:5; Eph. 1:6; 1 John 1:3.

Q. 33. Why do we call Him our Lord?

A. Because He, redeeming and ransoming both our body and soul from sin, not with gold or silver, but with His precious blood, and delivering us from all the power of the devil, has set us free to serve Him (a).
(a) Rom. 14:9; 1 Cor. 6:20; Eph. 1:7; 1 Tim. 2:5-6; 1 Pet. 1:18.

Q. 34. What do you believe when you say He was conceived by the Holy Spirit, and born of the virgin Mary?

A. That the Son of God, who is and continues true and everlasting God (a), took the very nature of man (b), of the flesh and blood of the virgin Mary (c), through the working of the Holy Spirit (d), that He might be the true Seed of David (e), like unto His brethren in all things, sin excepted (f).
(a) John 20:28; Rom. 9:5; 1 John 5:20.
(b) Isa. 7:14; 9:6; John 1:14.
(c) Gal. 4:4.
(d) Matt. 1:20.
(e) Rom. 1:3.
(f) Phil. 2:7; Heb. 4:15; 7:26.

Q. 35. What profit do you take by Christ's holy conception and nativity?

A. That He is our Mediator, and does cover with His innocence and perfect holiness my sins (a), in which I was conceived, that they may not come in the sight of God (b).
(a) Heb. 2:16-17; 4:15.
(b) Psa. 32:1; Rom. 8:3-4; 1 Cor. 1:30; Rom. 8:3-4.

Q. 36. What do you believe when you say He suffered?

A. That He all the time of His life which He led on the earth, but especially at the end of it, sustained the wrath of God, both in body and soul (a), against the sin of all mankind, that

He might by His passion, as the only propitiatory sacrifice (b), deliver our body and soul from everlasting damnation and purchase for us the favor of God, righteousness, and eternal life.
(a) Isa. 53:12; 1 Pet. 2:4; 3:18.
(b) 1 John 2:2; 4:10.

Q. 37. For what cause should He suffer under Pilate, as being His judge?

A. That He being innocent (a) and condemned before a civil judge (b), might deliver us from the severe judgment of God which remained for all men (c).
(a) Luke 23:14; John 19:4.
(b) Psa. 69:4; John 15:25.
(c) Isa. 53:4-5; 2 Cor. 5:21; Gal. 3:13.

Q. 38. But is there any more in it, that He was fastened to the cross, than if He had suffered any other kind of death?

A. There is more. By this I am assured that He took upon Himself the curse which did lie on me, for the death of the cross was cursed of God (a).
(a) Deut. 21:23; Gal. 3:13.

Q. 39. Why was it necessary for Christ to humble Himself unto death?

A. Because the justice and truth of God could by no other means be satisfied for our sins (a), but by the very death of the Son of God (b).
(a) Gen. 2:17.
(b) Phil. 2:8; Heb. 2:9, 14-18.

Q. 40. To what end was He buried?

A. That by it He might manifest that He was dead indeed (a).
(a) Matt. 27:59- 60; Luke 23:53; John 19:38; Acts 13:29.

Q. 41. But since Christ died for us, why must we also die?

A. Our death is not a satisfaction for our sins, but the abolishing of sin and our passage into everlasting life (a).
(a) John 5:24; Rom. 7:24; Phil. 1:23.

Q. 42. What other benefit do we receive by the death of Christ?

A. That by virtue of His death our old man is crucified, slain, and buried together with Him (a), figured out in holy baptism, that henceforth evil lusts and desires may not reign in us (b), but we may offer ourselves unto Him a sacrifice of thanksgiving (c).
(a) Rom. 6:6.
(b) Rom. 6:12.
(c) Rom. 12:1.

Q. 43. Why is there added, "He descended into hell"?

A. That in my greatest pains and most grievous temptations I may support myself with this comfort, that my Lord Jesus Christ has delivered me (by the unspeakable distresses, torments, and terrors of His soul, into which He was plunged both before and then especially when He hung on the cross) from the straits and torments of hell (a).

(a) Isa. 53:10; Matt. 27:46. Not that He (that is, Christ) went into the place of the damned, but that He went absolutely into the place of the dead. See Dr. Usher in his *Body of Divinity*, 174 and Mr. Perkins on the Creed.

Q. 44. What does the resurrection of Christ profit us?

A. First, by His resurrection, He vanquished death (a), that He might make us partakers of that righteousness which He had gotten us by His death. Second, we are now also stirred up by His power to a new life (b). Lastly, the resurrection of our head, Christ, is a pledge to us of our glorious resurrection (c).

(a) Rom. 4:25; 1 Pet. 1:3-4, 21.
(b) Rom. 6:4; Col. 3:1.
(c) Rom. 8:11; 1 Cor. 15:22-23.

Q. 45. How do you understand that He ascended into heaven?

A. That Christ, His disciples looking on, was taken up from the earth into heaven (a), and yet still is there for our sakes (b), and will be until He comes again to judge the living and the dead (c).

(a) Mark 16:19; Luke 24:51; Acts 1:9.
(b) Rom. 8:34; Eph. 4:10; Col. 3:1; Heb. 4:14; 7:25; 9:11.
(c) Matt. 24:30; Acts 1:11.

Q. 46. Is not Christ with us then until the end of the world, as He has promised?

A. Christ is true God, and true man, and so according to His manhood is not now on earth (a), but according to His Godhead, His majesty, His grace and Spirit is at no time apart from us (b).

(a) Matt. 26:11; John 16:18; 17:11; Acts 3:21.
(b) Matt. 28:20; John 14:17; 16:13; Eph. 4:8.

Q. 47. Are not by this means the two natures in Christ pulled apart, if His humanity be not wherever His divinity is?

A. No. Seeing His divinity is incomprehensible, and everywhere present (a), it follows necessarily that the same is without the bounds of His human nature which He took to Himself, and yet is nevertheless in it, and abides personally united to it (b).

(a) Jer. 23:23-24; Acts 7:48-49; 17:27.
(b) Matt. 28:6; Col. 2:9.

Q. 48. What fruit does the ascension of Christ into heaven bring to us?

A. First, that He makes intercession to His Father in heaven for us (a). Second, that we have our flesh in heaven, that we may be confirmed thereby, as by a sure pledge, that He who is our head will lift us up (b), His members, unto Him. Third, that He sends us His Spirit as a pledge between Him and us (c), by whose power we seek after not earthly but heavenly things (d), where He Himself is sitting at the right hand of God (e).
(a) Rom. 8:34; 1 John 2:1-2.
(b) John 14:2; 20:17; Eph. 2:6.
(c) John 14:16; 16:7; 2 Cor. 5:5; Eph. 1:13-14.
(d) Phil. 3:14; Col. 3:1.
(e) Eph. 1:20; Phil. 3:20.

Q. 49. Why is it further said, "He sits at the right hand of God"?

A. Because Christ is ascended into heaven, to show there that He is the head of His Church (a), by whom the Father governs all things (b).
(a) Eph. 1:20-23; 5:23; Col. 1:18.
(b) Matt. 28:18; John 5:22.

Q. 50. What profit is this glory of our head Christ to us?

A. First, that through His Holy Spirit, He pours upon us, His

members, heavenly graces (a), and that He shields and defends us by His power against all our enemies (b).
(a) Eph. 4:16.
(b) Psa. 2:9; 110:2; John 10:28; Eph. 4:8.

Q. 51. What comfort do you have by the coming of Christ again to judge the living and the dead?

A. That in all my miseries and persecutions, I look with my head lifted up (a), for the very same who before yielded Himself to the judgment of God for me, and took away all malediction from me, will come as judge from heaven to throw all His and my enemies into everlasting pains (b). He will also translate me with all His chosen to Himself, into celestial joys, and everlasting glory (c).
(a) Luke 21:28; Rom. 8:23; Phil. 3:20; Titus 2:13.
(b) Matt. 25:41; 2 Thess. 1:6-10.
(c) Matt. 25:34; 1 Thess. 4:16-18; Jude 24-25.

Chapter 5

The Second Part: Of Man's Redemption (God the Holy Spirit)

God the Holy Spirit

Q. 52. What do you believe concerning the Holy Spirit?

A. First, that He is true and coeternal God, with the eternal Father and the Son (a). Second, that He is also given unto me (b), to make me partaker of Christ and all His benefits through a true faith (c), to comfort me (d), and to abide with me forever (e).
(a) Gen. 1:2; Isa. 48:16; Matt. 28:19; Acts 5:3-4; 1 Cor. 3:16; 6:19.
(b) John 14:16.
(c) 1 Cor. 6:17; 1 Pet. 1:2; 4.
(d) Acts 9:31.
(e) John 14:16; 1 Pet. 4:14.

Q. 53. What do you believe concerning the holy and catholic

Church of Christ?

A. I believe that the Son of God does (a), from the beginning to the end of the world (b), gather, defend, and preserve for Himself, by His Spirit and Word (c), out of the whole of mankind (d), a company chosen to everlasting life (e), and agreeing in true faith (f); and that I am a lively member of that company (g), and so shall remain forever (h).
(a) Eph. 1:10-13.
(b) John 10:10; Rom. 3:25.
(c) Isa. 59:21; Matt. 16:18; Rom. 1:16; 10:14-17; Eph. 5:26.
(d) Gen. 26:4.
(e) Rom. 8:29-30.
(f) Matt. 16:16-18; Eph. 4:3-6.
(g) 2 Cor.13:5; 1 John 3:21.
(h) 1 John 5:20.

Q. 54. What do these words mean, the communion of saints?

A. First, that all and everyone who believes are in common partakers of Christ and all His graces (a), as being His members, and then that everyone ought readily and cheerfully to bestow the gifts and graces which they have received to the common commodity and safety of all (b).
(a) Rom. 8:32; 1 Cor. 1:2; 6:17; 12:21; 1 John 1:3.
(b) 1 Cor. 12:21; Phil. 2:4-6.

Q. 55. What do you believe concerning remission of sins?

A. That God, for the satisfaction made by Christ (a), has put out all the remembrance of my sins (b), and also of that corruption within me which I must fight all my lifetime, and does freely endow me the righteousness of Christ, that I come not at any time into judgment (c).

(a) 2 Cor. 5:19, 21; 1 John 2:2.
(b) Psa. 103:3-4; 10-12; Jer. 31:34; Rom. 7:24-25.
(c) John 3:18; Rom. 8:1-3.

Q. 56. What comfort do you have by the resurrection of the flesh?

A. That not only my soul, after it shall depart out of my body, shall presently be taken up to Christ (a), but that this my flesh also, being raised up by the power of Christ, shall again be united to my soul, and made like the glorious body of Christ (b).

(a) Luke 23:43; Phil. 1:23.
(b) Job 19:25-26; 1 Cor. 15:53; Phil. 3:21; 1 John 3:2.

Q. 57. What comfort do you take from the article of everlasting life?

A. That forasmuch as I feel already in my heart the beginning of everlasting life (a), it shall at length come to pass that after this life I shall enjoy full and perfect bliss (b), wherein I may magnify God forever, which blessedness surely neither eye has seen, nor ear heard, neither has any man in thought conceived it (c).

(a) 2 Cor. 5:1-3.
(b) John 17:3; Jude 24-25.
(c) 1 Cor. 2:9.

Q. 58. What profit is there to you when you believe all these things?

A. That I am righteous in Christ before God, and an heir of eternal life (a).
(a) John 3:36; Rom. 1:17; 3:22, 24, 25, 28; 5:1; Gal. 2:16; Eph. 2:8-9.

Q. 59. How are you righteous before God?

A. Only by faith in Christ Jesus. Although my conscience accuse me that I have grievously trespassed against all the commandments of God, and have not kept one of them (a), and further am as yet prone to all evil (b), yet nevertheless, if I embrace these benefits of Christ with a true confidence and persuasion of mind (c), the full and perfect satisfaction, righteousness, and holiness of Christ (d), without any merit of mine (e), of the mere mercy of God (f) is imputed and given to me (g), and that so, as if neither I had committed any sin, neither any corruption did stick to me, yes as if I myself had perfectly accomplished that obedience which Christ accomplished for me (h).
(a) Rom. 3:9.
(b) Rom. 7:23.
(c) John 3:18; Rom. 3:22.

(d) 1 John 2:1.
(e) Rom. 3:24; Eph. 2:8-9; 1 John 2:2.
(f) Titus 3:5.
(g) Rom. 4:4-5; 2 Cor. 5:19.
(h) 2 Cor. 5:21.

Q. 60. Why do you affirm that you are made righteous by faith only?

A. Not because I please God through the worthiness of mere faith, but because only the satisfaction, righteousness, and holiness of Christ is my righteousness before God (a), and I cannot take hold of it, or apply it to myself any other way than by faith (b).
(a) 1 Cor. 1:30; 2:2.
(b) 1 John 5:10.

Q. 61. Why can't our good works be righteousness, or some part of righteousness, before God?

A. Because the righteousness which must stand fast before the judgment of God, must be in all points perfect and agreeable to the law of God (a). Now our works, even the best of them, are imperfect in this life, and defiled with sin (b).
(a) Deut. 27:26; Gal. 3:10.
(b) Isa. 64:6.

Q. 62. How is it that our good works merit nothing, seeing

The Second Part: Of Man's Redemption (God the Holy Spirit)

God promises that He will give a reward for them both in this life and in the life to come?

A. That reward is not given of merit, but of grace (a).
(a) Luke 17:10.

Q. 63. But does not this doctrine make men careless and profane?

A. No. Those who are incorporated into Christ through faith, necessarily bring forth the fruits of thankfulness (a).
(a) Matt. 7:18; John 15:5.

The Second Part: Of Man's Redemption (God the Holy Spirit)

Chapter 6

The Second Part:

Of Man's Redemption

(The Sacraments)

The Sacraments

Q. 64. Since faith alone makes us partakers of Christ and His benefits, from where does this faith come?

A. From the Holy Spirit (a), who kindles it in our hearts by the preaching of the gospel (b), and other ordinances (c), and confirms it by the use of the sacraments (d).
(a) John 3:5; Eph. 2:8; 3:16-17; Phil.1:29.
(b) Rom. 10:17.
(c) Eph. 3:16-17; Heb. 4:16.
(d) 1 Cor. 10:16; 1 Pet. 3:21.

Q. 65. What are the sacraments?

A. They are sacred signs and seals set before our eyes and

74 | *An Orthodox Catechism*

ordained of God for this purpose, that He may declare and confirm by them the promise of His gospel unto us, to this, that He gives freely remission of sins and life everlasting to everyone in particular who believes in the sacrifice of Christ which He accomplished once for all upon the cross (a).
(a) Matt. 28:19-20; 1 Cor. 10:16; Rom. 6:3-6; Heb. 10:10.

Q. 66. Do not then both the Word and sacraments tend to that end, to lead our faith to the sacrifice of Christ finished on the cross as the only ground of our salvation?

A. It is even so. The Holy Spirit teaches us by the gospel, and assures us by the sacraments that the salvation of all of us stands in the once for all sacrifice of Christ offered for us upon the cross (a).
(a) Rom. 6:3; 1 Cor. 11:23-26; Gal. 3:27.

Q. 67. How many sacraments has Christ ordained in the New Testament?

A. Two. Baptism and the Lord's Supper.

The Second Part: Of Man's Redemption (The Sacraments)

Chapter 7

The Second Part: Of Man's Redemption (Baptism)

Baptism

Q. 68. What is baptism?

A. Immersion or dipping of the person in water in the name of the Father, Son, and Holy Spirit, by such who are duly qualified by Christ (a).
(a) Matt. 3:16; 28:19-20; John 3:23; Acts 8:38-39; Rom. 6:4.

Q. 69. Who are the proper subjects of this ordinance?

A. Those who do actually profess repentance towards God, and faith in and obedience to our Lord Jesus Christ (a).
(a) Acts 2:38; 8:36-37.

Q. 70. Are infants to be baptized?

A. None by no means, for we have neither precept nor example for that practice in all the book of God.

Q. 71. Do the Scriptures anywhere expressly forbid the baptism of infants?

A. It is sufficient that the divine oracle commands the baptizing of believers (a), unless we will make ourselves wiser than what is written. Nadab and Abihu were not forbidden to offer strange fire, yet for so doing they incurred God's wrath, because they were commanded to take fire from the altar (b).
(a) Matt. 28:18-19; Mark 16:16.
(b) Lev. 9:24; 10:1-3.

Q. 72. May the infant seed of believers under the gospel be baptized just as the infant seed of Abraham under the law was circumcised?

A. No. Abraham had a command then from God to circumcise his infant seed, but believers have no command to baptize their infant seed under the gospel.
(a) Gen. 17:9-12.

Q. 73. Since some say that the infants of believers are in the covenant of grace with their parents, why may they not be baptized under the gospel, just as Abraham's infant seed was circumcised under the law?

A. By asserting that the infants of believers are in the covenant of grace, they must either mean of the covenant of grace absolutely considered, and if so, then there is no total and final apostasy of any infant seed of believers from the covenant, but all must be saved then (a).
(a) Jer. 32:38-40; John 10:28.

Or, they must mean conditionally, that when they come to years of maturity, they by true faith, love, and holiness of life, taking hold of God's covenant of grace, shall have the privileges of it. If this is their meaning, then what spiritual privilege does the infant seed of believers have more than the infant seed of unbelievers, if they live also to years of maturity, and by true faith and love take hold God's covenant? Furthermore, would not the seal of the covenant belong as much to the children of unbelievers as to the children of believers? Yes, since the infant seed of the unbeliever sometimes comes to embrace God's covenant, and the infant seed of the believer does not; as often this is seen to the sorrow of many godly parents (b).
(b) Isa. 56:3-8; John 3:16; Acts 10:34-35.

Suppose all the infant seed of believers are absolutely in the covenant of grace; yet believers under the gospel ought no more to baptize their infant seed than Lot to circumcise himself or his infant seed, if he had males as well as females, although he was related to Abraham, a believer, and in the covenant of grace, since circumcision was limited to Abraham and his immediate family. If the infant seed of believers are absolutely in the covenant of grace, we may bring infants to the Lord's Table because the same qualifications are required

The Second Part: Of Man's Redemption (Baptism)

to the due performance of baptism as for the Lord's Supper (c).
(c) Acts 2:41-42.

The covenant made with Abraham had two parts:

First, a spiritual component, which consisted in God's promising to be a God to Abraham and all his spiritual seed in a peculiar manner (d), whether they were circumcised or uncircumcised, who believed as Abraham the father of the faithful did (e). And this was signified in God's accepting such as His people which were not of Abraham's seed, but bought with his money, and this promise was sealed to Abraham by circumcision, that through Jesus Christ (whom Isaac typified) the Gentiles, the uncircumcision which believed (f), should have their faith counted for righteousness, as Abraham's was before he was circumcised (g).
(d) Gen. 17:19, 21; 21:10; Gal. 4:30.
(e) Acts 2:39; Rom. 9:7-8.
(f) Gal. 3:16, 28-29.
(g) Rom. 4:9-14.

Second, this promise consisted of a temporal component. Thus, God promised Abraham's seed should enjoy the land of Canaan, and have plenty of outward blessings (h), so He sealed this promise by circumcision (i). Circumcision also distinguished the Jews as being God's people from all the nations of the Gentiles, which as yet were not the seed of Abraham. But when the Gentiles came to believe and by faith became the people of God as well as the Jews, then circumcision, that distinguishing mark, ceased. The distinguishing mark of being the children of God now is faith in Christ and circumcision of the heart (j). Therefore, whatever pretence there may be to baptize the infants of believers avails nothing, whether their being the seed of believers, their being in the covenant, or that the infant seed of Abraham, a believer, was circumcised. Circumcision was limited also to the family of Abraham, all others, though believers, being excluded. Circumcision was limited also to the eighth day, and whatever pretence might be made, it was not to be done before nor after. It was limited to males, which if baptism came in the room of circumcision and is the seal of the covenant under the gospel, as circumcision was under the law, none but males must be baptized. Just as under the law circumcision had peculiar regulations, so it is under the gospel concerning baptism. These regulations concerning baptism depend purely upon the will of the Lawgiver, that Prophet to whom we would do well to listen (k). He determines upon whom, when, and how baptism is to be administered.

(h) Gen. 12:6-7; 13:15-17; 15:16, 18.
(i) Gen. 17:8-11.
(j) John 1:12; Rom. 2:28-29; Gal. 3:26-28; Phil. 3:3.
(k) Acts 3:22.

Q. 74. How are you admonished and assured in baptism that you are a partaker of the only sacrifice of Christ?

A. Because Christ commanded the outward washing of water (a), joining this promise to it, that I am no less assuredly

washed by His blood and Spirit from all uncleanness of my soul, that is, from all my sins (b), than I am washed outwardly from the filthiness of the body with water.
(a) Matt. 28:19; Acts 2:38.
(b) Matt. 3:11; Mark 1:4; 16:16; Luke 3:3; Rom. 6:3.

Q. 75. What is it to be washed with the blood and Spirit of Christ?

A. It is to receive of God forgiveness of sins freely, for the blood of Christ which He shed for us in His sacrifice upon the cross (a) and also to be renewed by the Holy Spirit, and through His sanctifying of us to become members of Christ, that we may more and more die to sin, and live holy and without blame (b).
(a) Ezek. 36:25; Zech. 13:1; Heb. 12:24; 1 Pet. 1:2; Rev. 1:5.
(b) John 1:33; 3:5; Rom. 6:4; 1 Cor. 6:11; 12:13; Col. 2:12.

Q. 76. Where does Christ promise us that He will as certainly wash us with His blood and Spirit as we are washed with the water of baptism?

A. In the institution of baptism, the words of which are these, go, teach all nations, baptizing them in the name of the Father, the Son, and the Holy Spirit (a); he that shall believe, and be baptized, shall be saved, but he that will not believe shall be damned (b). This promise is repeated again when the Scripture calls baptism the washing of the new birth (c), and forgiveness of sins (d).

(a) Matt. 28:19.
(b) Mark 16:16.
(c) Titus 3:5.
(d) Acts 22:16.

Q. 77. Is then the outward baptism in water the washing away of sins?

A. It is not (a). The blood of Christ alone cleanses us from all sin (b).
(a) Eph. 5:25-26; 1 Pet. 3:21.
(b) 1 Cor. 6:11; 1 John 1:7.

Q. 78. Why then does the Holy Spirit call baptism the washing of the new birth and forgiveness of sins?

A. God speaks so not without great cause, to this, not only to teach us that as the filth of our body is purged by water, so our sins also are purged by the blood and Spirit of Christ (a), but much more to assure us by this divine token and pledge that we are as surely washed from our sins with the inward washing as we are washed by the outward and visible water (b).
(a) 1 Cor. 6:11; Rev. 1:5; 7:14.
(b) Mark 16:16; Gal. 3:27.

Chapter 8

The Second Part: Of Man's Redemption (The Lord's Supper)

The Lord's Supper

Q. 79. How are you in the Lord's Supper admonished and warranted that you are a partaker of that only sacrifice of Christ offered on the cross and of all His benefits?

A. Because Christ has commanded me and all the faithful to eat of this bread broken and to drink of this cup distributed in remembrance of Him. With this He has joined the promise that His body was as certainly broken and offered for me upon the cross and His blood shed for me as I behold with my eyes the bread of the Lord broken to me and the cup communicated to me. Further, my soul is no less assuredly fed to everlasting life with His body, which was crucified for me, and His blood, which was shed for me, than I receive and taste by the mouth of my body the bread and wine, the signs of the body and blood of the Lord, received at the hand of the minister (a).

(a) Matt. 26:27-28; Mark 14:22-24; Luke 22:16, 20; 1 Cor. 10:16-17; 11:23-25; 12:13.

Q. 80. What is it to eat of the body of Christ?

A. It is not only to embrace, by an assured confidence of mind, the whole passion and death of Christ and thereby to obtain forgiveness of sins and everlasting life (a), but also by the Holy Spirit, who dwells both in Christ and us, so more and more to be united to His sacred body (b), that though He be in heaven and we on earth (c), yet nevertheless we are flesh of His flesh and bone of His bones (d). As all the members of the body are quickened by one soul, so are we also quickened and guided by one and the same Spirit (e).

(a) John 6:35, 40, 47, 48, 50, 51, 53, 54.

(b) John 6:56.

(c) Acts 1:9; 3:21; 1 Cor. 11:26.

(d) John 14:23; 1 Cor. 6:15, 17, 19; Eph. 5:29, 30, 32; 1 John 3:24; 4.13.

(e) John 6:56-58; 15:1-6; Eph. 4:15-16.

Q. 81. Where has Christ promised that He will as certainly give His body and blood to be eaten and drank as they eat this bread broken and drink this cup?

A. In the institution of the Supper, the words of which are these:

Our Lord Jesus Christ in the night that He was betrayed, took bread, and when He had given thanks, He broke it, and said, take, eat, this is My body which is broken for you. This do in remembrance of Me. Likewise also He took the cup, when He had eaten, and said, this cup is the New Covenant in My blood. This do as often as you shall drink it in remembrance of Me. For as often as you shall eat this bread and drink this cup you show the Lord's death until He comes (a).
(a) Matt. 26:26ff.; Mark 14:22ff.; Luke 22:19; 1 Cor. 11:23ff.

This promise is repeated by St. Paul, where he says, the cup of blessing which we bless, is it not the communion of the blood of Christ? The bread which we break, is it not the communion of the body of Christ? For we that are many are one bread and one body, because we are all partakers of one bread (b).
(b) 1 Cor. 10:16-17.

Q. 82. Are then the bread and wine made the very body and blood of Christ?

A. No. As the water of baptism is not turned into the blood of Christ, but is only a sign and pledge of those things that are sealed to us in baptism, so neither is the bread of the Lord's Supper the very body of Christ, although according to the manner of sacraments and that form of speaking of them which is usual to the Holy Spirit, the bread is called the body of Christ (a).
(a) Matt. 26:28; Mark 14:24; 1 Cor. 10:16-17.

The Second Part: Of Man's Redemption (The Lord's Supper)

Q. 83. Why then does Christ call bread His body and the cup His blood, or the New Testament in His blood; and St. Paul calls bread and wine the communion of the body and blood of Christ?

A. Christ not without great consideration speaks in this manner, not only to teach us that as the bread and wine sustain the life of the body, so also His crucified body and shed blood are indeed the meat and drink of our souls, whereby they are nourished to eternal life (a). But more than that, by this visible sign and pledge, He may assure us that we are as surely partakers of His body and blood (b), through the working of the Holy Spirit as we do perceive by the mouth of our body these holy signs in remembrance of Him, and further also, that His sufferings and obedience is so certainly ours, as though we ourselves had suffered punishments for our sins, and had satisfied God.
(a) John 6:51, 55, 56.
(b) 1 Cor. 10:16-17.

Q. 84. What difference is there between the Supper of the Lord and the Popish mass?

A. The Supper of the Lord testifies to us that we have perfect forgiveness of all our sins, on account of the only sacrifice of Christ, which He once fully wrought on the cross (a). It also testifies that we, by faith, are grafted into Christ (b), who now according to His human nature is only in heaven at the right hand of His Father (c), and there will be worshipped by us (d). But in the mass it is denied that the living and the dead have remission of sins by the only passion of Christ, except He also be daily offered for them by their sacrifices. Further, it is taught that Christ is bodily under the forms of bread and wine, and therefore is to be worshipped in them and so the very foundation of the mass is nothing else but an utter denial of that only sacrifice and passion of Christ Jesus, and an accursed idolatry.

(a) Matt. 26:28; Luke 22:19-20; John 19:30; Heb. 7:27; 9:12, 26, 28; 10:10, 12, 14.

(b) 1 Cor. 6:17; 10:16-17; 12:13.

(c) Luke 24:5; John 20:17; Acts 7:55-56; Phil. 3:20; Col. 3:1; 1 Thess. 1:9-10; Heb. 1:3.

(d) John 4:21-24; Heb. 1:6, 8.

Q. 85. Who are to come to the table of the Lord?

A. They only who are truly sorrowful they have offended God by their sins, and yet trust that those sins are pardoned them for Christ's sake, and what other infirmities they have, that those are covered by His passion and death, who also desire more and more to go forward in faith and integrity of life. But hypocrites, and those who do not truly repent, do eat and drink damnation to themselves (a).

(a) 1 Cor. 10:21-22; 11:27ff.

Q. 86. Are they also to be admitted to the Lord's Supper who in confession and life declare themselves to be infidels, profane, and ungodly?

A. No. By that means the ordinance of God is profaned and the wrath of God is stirred up against the whole assembly (a), wherefore the church by the commandment of Christ and His Apostles, inspired by the Holy Spirit, using the keys of the kingdom of heaven, ought to drive them from this Supper till they shall repent and change their manners.
(a) 1 Cor. 11:20-22, 34; Cf. Psa. 50:1ff; Isa. 1:11ff; 66:3; Jer. 7:21ff.

Q. 87. How ought this ordinance of the Lord's Supper to be closed?

A. In singing praises to God vocally and audibly for His great benefits and blessings to His Church in the shedding of the most precious blood of His Son to take away their sin, which blessings are pointed out in this sacrament. Also, we find our Lord and His disciples concluded this ordinance in singing a hymn or psalm (a). If Christ sang, who was going to die, how much more cause to sing have we for whom He died. He died that we might not eternally die, but live a spiritual and eternal life with Father, Son, and Spirit in inexpressible glory.
(a) Matt. 26:30.

Q. 88. You told us but now, that those who in confession and life declare themselves to be infidels, profane and ungodly, should by the keys of the kingdom of heaven be driven from this Supper. What are the keys of the kingdom of heaven?

A. The preaching of the gospel and ecclesiastical discipline,

by which heaven is opened to the believers, and is shut against the unbelievers (a).
(a) Matt. 16:19; 18:18.

Q. 89. How is the kingdom of heaven opened and shut by the preaching of the gospel?

A. The kingdom of heaven is opened when, by the commandment of Christ, it is publicly declared to everyone who believes that all their sins are pardoned by God due to the merit of Christ, as they embrace by a lively faith the promise of the gospel. But to the contrary, the kingdom of heaven is shut when it is announced to all infidels and hypocrites that as long as the wrath of God abides upon them, they perish in their wickedness, according to which testimony of the gospel God will judge them in this life and also in the life to come (a).
(a) Job 20:21-23; Matt. 16:19; John 12:48.

Q. 90. How is the kingdom of heaven opened and shut by ecclesiastical discipline?

A. The kingdom of heaven is shut when, according to the commandments of Christ, those who profess to be Christians, but who, in their doctrine and life, show themselves aliens from Christ, and after being admonished, will not depart from their error, heresies, or wickedness, are made known to the church. If they do not obey the church's admonition, they are by the same church to be kept from the sacrament and shut out of the congregation by authority received from Christ, and by God Himself shut out of the kingdom of heaven (a).

(a) Matt. 18:15-17; 1 Cor. 5:3-5; 2 Thess. 3:14-15.

The kingdom of heaven is opened if such persons as above profess and declare an amendment of life, nothing to the contrary being able to be proved upon strict scrutiny and search. These are to be received again in love and tenderness as members of Christ and His church (b).

(b) 2 Cor. 2:6-7, 10, 11.

Chapter 9

The Third Part: Of Man's Thankfulness (Introductory Questions)

THE THIRD PART
Of Man's Thankfulness

Q. 91. Whereas we are delivered from all our sins and miseries without any merit of ours, by the mercy of God, only for Christ's sake, for what cause are we to do good works?

A. Because, after Christ has redeemed us with His blood, He renews us also by His Spirit to the image of Himself, that we, receiving so great benefits, should show ourselves all our lifetime thankful to God, and honor Him (a); secondly that every one of us be assured of his faith by his fruit (b); and lastly, that by our good conversation we may win others to Christ (c).

(a) Rom. 6:1-4; 12:1-2; 1 Cor. 6:20; 1 Pet. 2:5, 9, 12.
(b) Matt. 7:17-18; Gal. 5:22; 2 Pet. 1:10.
(c) Matt. 5:16; 1 Pet. 3:1-2.

Q. 92. Can they be saved who are unthankful, and remain still careless in their sins, and are not converted from their wickedness to God?

A. By no means; for as the Scripture bears witness, neither unchaste persons, nor idolaters, nor adulterers, nor thieves, nor covetous, nor drunkards, nor slanderers, nor robbers, shall enter into the kingdom of God (a).
(a) 1 Cor. 6:9-10; Eph. 5:5-6; 1 John 3:14-15.

Q. 93. In how many things does true repentance toward or conversion to God consist?

A. It consists of the dying or mortifying of the old man and the renewing or quickening of the new man (a).
(a) Rom. 6:4-6; 1 Cor. 5:7; 2 Cor. 7:11; Eph. 4:22-24; Col. 3:5-10.

Q. 94. What is the dying or mortifying of the old man?

A. To be truly and heartily sorry that you have offended God by your sins and daily more and more hate and avoid them (a).
(a) Joel 2:13; Rom. 8:13.

Q. 95. What is the renewing or quickening of the new man?

A. True joy in God through Christ (a), and an earnest desire to order your life according to God's will and to do all good

works (b).
(a) Rom. 5:1; 14:17.
(b) Rom. 6:10-11; 12:1-2; Gal. 2:20.

Q. 96. What are good works?

A. Those only which are done by a true faith (a), according to God's law (b), and are referred only to His glory (c), and not those which are imagined by us as seeming to be right and good (d), or which are delivered and commanded by men (e).
(a) Rom. 14:23.
(b) 1 Sam. 15:22.
(c) 1 Cor. 10:31.
(d) Eph. 2:10.
(e) Deut. 11:32; Isa. 29:13; Ezek. 20:18-19; Matt. 15:9.

Chapter 10

The Third Part:
Of Man's Thankfulness
(The Law of God)

The Law of God

Q. 97. What is the law of God?

A. The Decalogue or Ten Commandments (a).
(a) Exod. 20; Deut. 5.

Q. 98. How are these commandments divided?

A. Into two tables (a), whereof the former, delivered in four commandments, tells us how we ought to behave ourselves towards God; the latter, delivered in six commandments, tells us what duties we owe to our neighbors (b).
(a) Exod. 34:28; Deut. 4:13; 10:3-4.
(b) Matt. 22:37-39.

96 | An Orthodox Catechism

Q. 99. What is the preface to the Ten Commandments?

A. I am Jehovah, the Lord your God, which brought you out of the land of Egypt, out of the house of bondage.

Q. 100. What do we learn from the preface?

A. Three things: first, He shows to whom the right of all rule belongs, that is, to God Himself, for I am (says He) Jehovah; secondly, He says, He is the God of His people, that through the promise of His bountifulness He might allure them to obey Him; and thirdly, He says, which brought you out of the land of Egypt, as if He should say, I am He who has manifested Myself to you and bestowed all those blessings upon you, therefore you are bound to show thankfulness and obedience to Me (a).
(a) Exod. 20:2.

Q. 101. Do these things belong to us?

A. They do, because they figuratively comprehend and imply all the deliverances of the Church; and further, this was a type of our wonderful deliverance achieved by Christ.

Q. 102. What is the first commandment?

A. You shall have no other Gods before Me.

The Third Part: Of Man's Thankfulness (The Law of God)

Q. 103. What does God require in the first commandment?

A. That as dearly as I render the salvation of my own soul, so earnestly should I shun and flee all idolatry (a), sorcery (b), enchantments, superstitions, praying to saints, or any other creatures (c), and should rightly acknowledge the only and true God (d), trust in Him alone (e), submit and subject myself to Him with all humility (f) and patience (g), look for all good things from Him alone (h), and lastly with the entire affection of my heart love, reverence, and worship Him (i), so that I am ready to renounce and forsake all creatures rather than to commit the least thing that may be against His will (j).

(a) 1 Cor. 6:9-10; 10:7, 14.
(b) Lev. 19:31; Deut. 18:11.
(c) Matt. 4:10; Rev. 19:10; 22:8-9.
(d) John 17:3.
(e) Jer. 17:5.
(f) 1 Pet. 5:5-6.
(g) Rom. 5:3-4; 1 Cor. 10:10; Phil. 2:14; Col. 1:11; Heb. 10:36.
(h) Isa. 45:7; James 1:17.
(i) Deut. 6:5; Psalm 10:4; Matt. 22:37.
(j) Deut. 6:2; Psa. 111:10; Matt. 4:20; 5:29; 10:37-38.

Q. 104. What is idolatry?

A. It is in place of that one God, or besides that one true God who has manifested Himself in His word and works, to make or imagine, and account any other thing in which I rest my hope and confidence (a).

(a) John 5:23; Gal. 4:8; Phil. 3:19; Eph. 2:12; 5:5; 1 John 2:23.

The Third Part: Of Man's Thankfulness (The Law of God)

Q. 105. What is the second commandment?

A. You shall not make any graven image, nor the likeness of anything which is in heaven above, or in the earth beneath, nor in the waters under the earth: you shall not bow down to them, nor worship them, for I the Lord your God am a jealous God, and visit the sins of the fathers upon the children, to the third and fourth generation of them that hate Me, and show mercy to thousands of them who love Me, and keep My commandments.

Q. 106. What does the second commandment require?

A. That we should not express or represent God by any image or shape and figure (a), or worship Him any other way than He has commanded in His word to be worshipped (b).
(a) Deut. 4:15ff.; Isa. 40:18ff.; Acts 17:29; Rom. 1:23ff.
(b) Deut. 12:30ff.; 1 Sam. 15:23; Matt. 15:9.

Q. 107. May any images or resemblances of God be made at all?

A. God neither ought, nor can be represented by any means. As for things created, although it is lawful to depict them, God nevertheless forbids their images to be made or possessed in order to worship or honor either them or God by them (a).
(a) Exod. 23:24; 34:13-14, 17; Num. 33:52; Deut. 7:5; 12:13; 16:22; 2 Kings 18:4.

The Third Part: Of Man's Thankfulness (The Law of God)

Chapter 10 | 99

Q. 108. But may not images be tolerated in churches, which may serve as books to the common people?

A. No, for that would make us wiser than God, who will have His church to be taught by the lively preaching of His word (a), and not with speechless images (b).
(a) 2 Tim. 3:16-17; 2 Pet. 1:19.
(b) Jer. 10:8ff.; Hab. 2:18-19.

Q. 109. What is the third commandment?

A. You shall not take the name of the Lord your God in vain, for the Lord will not hold him guiltless that takes His name in vain.

Q. 110. What does God require in the third commandment?

A. We must not use His name despitefully or irreverently, not only by cursing or false swearing (a), but also by unnecessary oaths (b). We must not be partakers of these horrible sins in others either by silence or consent. We must always use the sacred and holy name of God with great devotion and reverence (c), that He may be worshipped and honored by us with a true and steadfast confession and invocation of His name (d). This should be the case in all our words and actions (e).
(a) Lev. 19:12; 24:11ff.
(b) Matt. 5:37; James 5:12.
(c) 1 Tim. 2:8.

The Third Part: Of Man's Thankfulness (The Law of God)

(d) Matt. 10:32.
(e) Rom. 2:24; Col. 3:17; 1 Tim. 6:1.

Q. 111. Is taking God's name in vain by swearing or cursing so grievous a sin that God is also angry with those who do not forbid or hinder it with all their ability?

A. Surely it is most grievous (a). There is no sin greater or more offending to God than the despising of His sacred name, wherefore He even commanded this sin to be punished with death (b).
(a) Lev. 5:1.
(b) Lev. 24:15-16.

Q. 112. May a man swear reverently by the name of God?

A. Yes, he may when lawful magistrates or necessity require it. By this means the faith and truth of any man, or thing to be ratified and established, both the glory of God may be advanced and the safety of others procured. This kind of swearing is ordained by God's word (a), and therefore was well-used by the fathers both in the Old and New Testament (b).
(a) Deut. 6:13; 10:20; Isa. 48:1; Heb. 6:16.
(b) Gen. 21:24; 31; Josh. 9:15, 19; 2 Sam. 3:35; 1 Kings 1:29; Rom. 1:9.

Q. 113. Is it lawful to swear by saints or other creatures?

The Third Part: Of Man's Thankfulness (The Law of God)

A. No. A lawful oath is an invocation of God, whereby we desire that He, as the only searcher of hearts, bear witness to the truth and punish the swearer if he knowingly swears falsely (a). No creature deserves this honor (b).
(a) 2 Cor. 1:23.
(b) Matt. 5:34-36; James 5:12.

Q. 114. What is the fourth commandment?

A. Remember that you keep holy the Sabbath Day. You shall labor six days and do all your work, but the seventh day is the Sabbath of the Lord your God. In it you should do no manner of work, you, nor your son, nor your daughter, nor your man-servant, nor your maid-servant, nor your cattle, nor the stranger that is within your gates. For in six days the Lord made heaven and earth, the sea, and all that is in them, and rested the seventh day, and hallowed it.

Q. 115. What are we taught by the fourth commandment?

A. That one day in seven be kept in the worship of God. Under the Old Testament this was the last day of the week, but under the gospel changed to the first day of the week. The Lord's Day is to be spent in private and public devotion, hearing the word diligently, practicing the gospel-sacraments zealously, doing deeds of charity conscionably, and resting from servile works, except for cases of necessity. This was the laudable practice of the holy Apostles, who best knew the mind of Christ as to the time of worship. We do not

find in all the New Testament that any gospel church in the Apostle's time set any other day apart solemnly to worship God but the first day. This they were right to do. For if Israel, the natural seed of Abraham, was to keep the seventh day to keep up the remembrance of their deliverance out of temporal bondage, how much more are we bound to keep the first day in remembrance of Christ's deliverance of us from eternal bondage (a).
(a) Deut. 5:15; Psa. 40:9-10; Isa. 66:23; John 20:19-20; Acts 2:42, 46; 20:7; 1 Cor. 11:33; 14:16, 19, 29, 31; 16:1-2; 1 Tim. 2:1-3, 8-9; Rev. 1:10.

Q. 116. What is the fifth commandment?

A. Honor your father and mother that your days may be long in the land which the Lord your God gives you.

Q. 117. What does God require of us in the fifth commandment?

A. That we yield due honor, love, and faithfulness to our parents, and to all who have authority over us, and submit ourselves with such obedience as is fitting to their faithful commandments and chastisements (a). And that by our patience, we endure their mannerisms (b), thinking within ourselves that God will govern and guide us by them (c).
(a) Exod. 21:17; Prov. 1:8; 4:1; 15:20; 20:20; Rom. 13:1; Eph. 5:22; 6:1-2, 5; Col. 3:20, 22-24.
(b) Prov. 23:22; 1 Pet. 2:18.

The Third Part: Of Man's Thankfulness (The Law of God)

(c) Matt. 22:21; Rom. 13:1; Col. 3:18-25.

Q. 118. What is the sixth commandment?

A. You shall do no murder.

Q. 119. What does God require in the sixth commandment?

A. That neither in thought or in gesture, much less in deed, I reproach, or hate, or harm, or kill my neighbor, either by myself, or by another and that I cast away all desire of revenge (a). Furthermore, that I do not hurt myself or knowingly cast myself into any danger (b). God has armed the magistrate with the sword as a deterrent to murder (c).
(a) Matt. 5:21-22; 18:35; 26:52; Rom. 12:19; Eph. 4:26.
(b) Matt. 4:7; Rom. 13:14; Col. 2:23.
(c) Gen. 9:6; Exod. 21:14; Matt. 26:52; Rom. 13:4.

Q. 120. But does this commandment forbid murder only?

A. No. In forbidding murder, God further teaches that He hates the root, namely, anger (a), envy (b), hatred (c), and desire for revenge, accounting them all as murder (d).
(a) Gal. 5:20-21; James 1:20.
(b) Rom. 1:29.
(c) 1 John 2:9, 11.
(d) Matt. 5:21-22; 1 John 3:15.

The Third Part: Of Man's Thankfulness (The Law of God)

Q. 121. Does this commandment only require that we harm no one?

A. No. When God condemns anger, envy, and hatred, He requires that we love our neighbor as ourselves (a). We must use tenderness, courtesy, patience, and mercy towards him (b). We must also protect him from whatever may be hurtful to him, as much as we are able (c). Indeed, we must be so affected in mind that we do not hesitate to do good even to our enemies (d).
(a) Matt. 7:12; 22:39.
(b) Matt. 5:5, 7; Luke 6:36; Rom. 12:10, 18; Gal. 6:1-2; Eph. 4:2.
(c) Exod. 23:5.
(d) Matt. 5:43-45; Rom. 12:20.

Q. 122. What is the seventh commandment?

A. You shall not commit adultery.

Q. 123. What is the meaning of the seventh commandment?

A. That God hates and abominates all sexual vileness and filthiness (a). Therefore, we must hate and detest the same (b). This also means that we must live temperately, modestly, and chastely, whether we are married or single (c).
(a) Lev. 18.
(b) Jude 22-23.
(c) 1 Cor. 7:1-5; 1 Thess. 4:3-4; Heb. 13:4.

The Third Part: Of Man's Thankfulness (The Law of God)

Q. 124. Does God forbid nothing else in this commandment but actual adultery and other external acts of sexual sin?

A. No. Since our bodies and souls are the temples of the Holy Spirit, God will have us keep both in purity and holiness (a). Therefore, deeds, gestures, words, thoughts, filthy lusts (b), and whatever entices us to these, are all forbidden (c).
(a) 1 Cor. 6:18-20.
(b) Matt. 5:27-28.
(c) Job 31:1; Psa. 39:1; Eph. 5:18.

Q. 125. What is the eighth commandment?

A. You shall not steal.

Q. 126. What does God forbid in the eighth commandment?

A. Not only those thefts (a) and robberies, which the magistrate ought to punish, but whatever evil tricks and devices where we seek after the goods of others and endeavor with force (b) or with some form of deceit to convey them to ourselves. These include false weights, false or uneven measurements, false advertisement, counterfeit money, exorbitant interest (c), or any other way or means of benefitting ourselves, which God has forbidden (d). To these we may add all covetousness (e) and the manifold waste and abusing of God's gifts.
(a) 1 Cor. 6:10.
(b) Ezek. 45:9.

The Third Part: Of Man's Thankfulness (The Law of God)

(c) Psa. 15:5; Luke 6:35.
(d) Deut. 25:13-15; Prov. 11:1; 16:11; 1 Cor. 5:10-13; 6:10; 1 Thess. 4:6.
(e) Prov. 5:15; Luke 3:14.

Q. 127. What are those things which God here commands?

A. That with my power, I help and further the commodities and profit of my neighbor, and that I so deal with him as I would desire to be dealt with myself (a). I am required to do my own work plainly and faithfully, that I may thereby help others who are distressed with any need or calamity (b).
(a) Matt. 7:12.
(b) Eph. 4:28.

Q. 128. What is the ninth commandment?

A. You shall not bear false witness against your neighbor.

Q. 129. What does the ninth commandment require?

A. That I bear no false witness against any man (a), neither falsify any man's words, nor backbite (b), nor reproach any man, nor condemn any rashly or unheard (c). I must avoid and shun with all carefulness all kinds of lies and deceits, as the proper works of the Devil (d), or I will stir up against me the most grievous wrath of God (e). In judgments and other affairs, I must follow the truth, and freely and constantly

profess the matter as it indeed is, as well as defend and increase, as much as in me lies, the good name and estimation of others (f).
(a) Prov. 19:5, 9; 21:28.
(b) Psa. 15:3; Rom. 1:29, 30.
(c) Matt. 7:1; Luke 6:37.
(d) John 8:44.
(e) Prov. 12:22; 13:5.
(f) Eph. 4:24-25; 1 Pet. 4:8.

Q. 130. What is the tenth commandment?

A. You shall not covet your neighbor's house, nor his wife, nor his servant, nor his maid, nor anything that is his (a).
(a) Exod. 20:17.

Q. 131. What does the tenth commandment forbid?

A. That our hearts be moved by the least desire or cogitation against any commandment of God, but that we continually, from our heart, detest all sin and delight in all righteousness (a).
(a) Rom. 7:7.

Q. 132. Can they who are converted to God observe and keep these commandments perfectly?

A. No. Even the holiest men, as long as they live, have only

small beginnings in obedience (a). Yet they begin with an unfeigned and earnest desire and endeavor to live not according to some, but all the commandments of God (b).
(a) Eccl. 7:22; Rom. 7:14-15; James 2:10.
(b) Rom. 7:22.

Q. 133. Why does God require His law to be preached exactly and severely, knowing that there is no man in this life able to keep it?

A. First, that we increasingly acknowledge the great proneness of our nature to sin and heartily desire forgiveness and righteousness in Christ (a). Second, that we do this always and so implore and crave from the Father the grace of His Holy Spirit (b). It is by this grace that we may be renewed, day by day, to the image and likeness of God (c). Once we depart out of this life, we will attain to that joyful perfection which is promised to us (d).
(a) Rom. 7:24; 1 John 1:9.
(b) Psa. 22:5; Luke 11:13; Eph. 3:16.
(c) 1 Cor. 9:24-27; Eph. 4:17-24; Phil. 3:12-14; Col. 3:5-14.
(d) Phil. 3:20-21; 1 John 3:2; Jude 24-25.

The Third Part: Of Man's Thankfulness (The Law of God)

Chapter 11

The Third Part:
Of Man's Thankfulness
(Prayer)

Prayer

Q. 134. Why is prayer necessary for Christians?

A. Because it is the chief part of thankfulness which God requires of us, and also because God gives His grace and Holy Spirit to those who with sincere groanings ask them continually of Him, and give Him thanks for them (a).
(a) Psa. 50:15; Matt. 7:7-8; Luke 11:9-13.

Q. 135. What is required for our prayers to please God and be heard by Him?

A. That we ask of the only true God, who has manifested Himself in His word (a), all things which He has commanded to be asked of Him (b). This is to be done with a true affection and desire of our heart (c). As well, we are, through an inward feeling of our need and misery, to cast ourselves prostrate in the presence of His divine majesty (d) and build ourselves on the sure foundation that we, though unworthy, yet for Christ's sake, are certainly heard by God (e), even as He has promised us in His word (f).

(a) John 4:22-24.
(b) Rom. 8:26; 1 John 5:14.
(c) Psa. 145:18.
(d) Psa. 2:11; 34:19; Isa. 66:2.
(e) Psa. 143:1; Rom. 8:15-16; 10:13-17; James 1:6ff.
(f) Dan. 9:17-19; John 14:13; 15:16; 16:23.

Q. 136. What are those things which God commands us to ask of Him?

A. All things necessary both for soul and body, which our Lord Jesus Christ has comprised in the prayer He taught us (a).

(a) Matt. 6:9-13; James 1:17.

Q. 137. What prayer is that?

A. Our Father who is in heaven, hallowed be Your name. Your kingdom come. Your will be done on earth, as it is in heaven. Give us this day our daily bread. And forgive us our trespasses, as we forgive those who trespass against us. And lead us not into temptation, but deliver us from evil. For Yours is the kingdom, the power, and the glory, forever and ever. Amen.

The Third Part: Of Man's Thankfulness (Prayer)

Q. 138. Are Christians tied to this very form of prayer?

A. We are not. Our Lord here delivers to His Church a brief summary of those things which we are to ask of God. Christ will have us also to ask for special things or particular benefits. The form prescribed is nothing else but a set of headings or general categories, wherein all benefits both bodily and spiritual are implied. But all particulars of prayer must agree and correspond with this general form. We are not tied to this form, as appears from James 1:5, where the Apostle exhorts the saints, if anyone lacks wisdom they should ask of God who gives to all liberally. Though these words are not in the form of prayer particularly expressed in the Lord's prayer, they are implied. Besides, we have examples of prayer both in the Old and New Testament, which are not in the form here expressed, though all they asked was comprehended in this prayer. Therefore, the form of prayer delivered to us by Christ is a thing indifferent.

Q. 139. Why does Christ teach us to call God our Father at the beginning of this prayer?

A. That He might stir up in us such a reverence and confidence in God as is proper for the sons of God. This must be the ground and foundation of our prayer; that is, that God through Christ is made our Father and will much less deny us these things which we ask of Him with a true faith than our earthly parents deny us earthly things (a).
(a) Matt. 7:9-11; Luke 11:11-13.

Q. 140. Why are the words "who is in heaven" added?

A. That we conceive not basely nor mundanely of God's heavenly majesty, and also that we look for and expect from His omnipotence whatever things are necessary for our soul and body (a).

(a) Jer. 23:24; Acts 17:24-27; Rom. 10:12.

Q. 141. What is the first petition?

A. Hallowed be Your name. In this we are asking that You would grant us, first to know You rightly (a) and worship, praise, and magnify Your almighty goodness, justice, mercy, and truth, which shine in all Your works (b). Also, we are asking You to direct our whole life, thoughts, words, and works to the end that Your most holy name be not reproached by us, but rather renowned with honor and praises (c).

(a) Psa. 119:105; Jer. 9:23-24; 31:33-34; Matt. 16:17; John 17:3; James 1:5.
(b) Exod. 34:5-7; Psa. 119:137-138; 143:1-2, 5, 10-12; 145:8-9, 17; Jer. 31:3; 32:18-19, 40-41; 33:11, 20-21; Matt. 19:17; Luke 1:45-55, 68-79; Rom. 3:3-4; 11:22-23; 2 Tim. 2:19.
(c) Psa. 115:1; 71:8.

Q. 142. What is the second petition?

A. Your kingdom come. In this we are asking that You would rule us by Your word and Spirit, that we may humble and

submit ourselves more and more to You (a). Also, we ask that You would preserve and increase Your Church (b), destroy the works of the Devil (c), and all power that lifts up itself against Your majesty. Make all those councils frustrated and void which are taken against Your word, until finally You reign fully and perfectly (d), when You shall be all in all (e).
(a) Psa. 119:5; 143:10; Matt. 6:33.
(b) Psa. 51:18; 122:6-7.
(c) Rom. 16:20; 1 John 3:8.
(d) Rom. 8:22-23; Rev. 22:17, 20.
(e) 1 Cor. 15:28.

Q. 143. What is the third petition?

A. Your will be done in earth, as it is in heaven. We are asking that You grant that we, and all men, renouncing and forsaking our own will (a), may readily and without any grudging (b), obey Your most holy will. This we pray that every one of us may faithfully perform that duty and charge which You have committed to us (c), even as the blessed angels do in heaven (d).
(a) Matt. 16:24; Tit. 2:12.
(b) Luke 22:42.
(c) 1 Cor. 7:24.
(d) Psa. 103:20-21.

Q. 144. What is the fourth petition?

A. Give us this day our daily bread. We ask that You give to us everything which is needful for this life, that by these things we may acknowledge and confess You to be the only fountain from where all good things flow (a). We also confess that all our care and industry, and even Your own gifts, are unfavorable and harmful to us unless You bless them (b). Grant that, turning our trust away from all creatures, we place and rest it in You alone (c).

(a) Psa. 10:4; 145:15-16; Matt. 6:25-34.
(b) Acts 14:16-17.
(c) Deut. 8:3; Psa. 27:13; 62:11.

Q. 145. Which is the fifth petition?

A. Forgive us our trespasses, as we forgive those who trespass against us. On the basis of the blood of Christ, do not impute unto us, most miserable and wretched sinners, any of our offences or the corruption which still cleaves to us (a). By Your grace in our hearts, we sincerely purpose to pardon and forgive all those who have offended us (b).

(a) Psa. 32:1-2; 143:2.
(b) Matt. 6:14.

Q. 146. What is the sixth petition?

A. Lead us not into temptation, but deliver us from evil. We are feeble and weak by nature (a) and cannot stand one moment without our most deadly enemies, Satan (b), the world (c), and our own flesh (d), incessantly attacking and assaulting us. Therefore, uphold, establish, and strengthen us by the might of Your Spirit that we may not in this spiritual combat yield as conquered, but withstand our enemies both stoutly and consistently (e), until we get the full and perfect victory (f).

(a) Psa. 103:14; John 15:5.
(b) Eph. 6:12; 1 Pet. 5:8.
(c) John 15:19.
(d) Rom. 7:23; Gal. 5:17.
(e) Matt. 26:41; Mark 13:33.
(f) 1 Thess. 3:13; 5:23.

Q. 147. How should you conclude this prayer?

A. For Yours is the kingdom, the power, and the glory forever. We ask and crave all these things of You because You are our King and almighty and are, therefore, both willing and able to give them to us (a). We ask these things that Your holy name alone may receive glory (b).

(a) Rom. 8:32; 10:11-12; 2 Pet. 2:9.
(b) Psa. 115:1; Jer. 33:8-9.

Q. 148. What does the final word, "Amen," mean?

A. That the thing is sure and not to be doubted. This is so because my prayer is much more certainly heard by God than I feel in my heart that I desire things from Him.

(a) 2 Cor. 1:20; 2 Tim. 2:13.

The Third Part: Of Man's Thankfulness (Prayer)

Chapter 12

The Nicene and Athanasian Creeds

The Nicene Creed, A.D. 325

We believe in one God, the Father Almighty, Maker of all things, visible and invisible. We believe in one Lord Jesus Christ, the Son of God, the only begotten Son of the Father, that is, of the substance of the Father, God of God, Light of Light, very God of very God, begotten, not made, being of one substance with the Father, by whom all things were made, both the things in heaven and the things in earth, who for us men and for our salvation came down and was incarnate. He was made man. He suffered and arose the third day. He ascended into heaven. He shall come to judge both the living and the dead. And we believe in the Holy Spirit. Those who say there was a time when the Son was not, therefore He was begotten, or He had His beginning of nothing, or that He is of another substance, or essence, or that affirm Him to be made, or to be changeable or mutable, these the Catholic and Apostolic Churches of God pronounce accursed.

The Athanasian Creed

Whoever will be saved before all things, it is necessary that he hold the catholic faith, which faith unless everyone do keep undefiled, without doubt he shall perish everlastingly.

And the catholic faith is this, that we worship one God in Trinity, and Trinity in unity, neither confounding the persons, nor dividing the substance.

For there is one person of the Father, another of the Son, and another of the Holy Spirit, but the Godhead of the Father, of the Son, of the Holy Spirit is all one, the glory equal, the majesty coeternal.

Such as the Father is, such is the Son, such is the Holy Spirit.

The Father uncreated, the Son uncreated, the Holy Spirit uncreated. The Father incomprehensible, the Son incomprehensible, the Holy Spirit incomprehensible.

The Father eternal, the Son eternal, the Holy Spirit eternal; yet are they not three eternals, but one eternal.

Also, there is not three incomprehensibles, nor three uncreated, but one uncreated, and one incomprehensible.

So likewise, the Father is almighty, the Son almighty, the Holy Spirit almighty, yet they are not three almighties, but one almighty.

So likewise the Father is Lord, the Son is Lord, the Holy Spirit is Lord; yet are they not three Lords, but one Lord.

For like as we are compelled by the Christian verity to acknowledge every person by Himself to be God and Lord, so are we forbidden by the catholic religion to say there be three Gods, or three Lords.

The Father is made of none, neither created, nor begotten. The Son is of the Father alone, not made, nor created, but begotten. The Holy Spirit is of the Father and the Son, neither made, nor created, nor begotten, but proceeding.

So there is one Father, not three Fathers; one Son, not three Sons; one Holy Spirit, not three Holy Spirits.

And in this Trinity none are before or after another, none is greater or less than another, but the whole three persons are coeternal and coequal. So that in all things, as is aforesaid, the unity in Trinity, and the Trinity in unity is to be worshiped.

He therefore that will be saved, must thus think of the Trinity.

Furthermore, it is necessary to everlasting life, that we also rightly believe the incarnation of our Lord Jesus Christ.

The Third Part: Of Man's Thankfulness (Prayer)

For the right faith is, that we believe and confess, that our Lord Jesus Christ, the Son of God, is God and man, God of the substance of the Father, begotten before the world, and man of the substance of His mother born in the world; perfect God, perfect man, of a reasonable soul and human flesh subsisting; equal to the Father as touching His Godhead, inferior to the Father as touching His manhood; who although He be God and man, yet is not two, but one Christ; one, not by conversion of the Godhead into flesh, but by taking of the manhood into God; one altogether not by confusion of substance, but by unity of Person. For as the reasonable soul and flesh is one man, so God and man is one Christ, who suffered for our salvation, descended into hell, rose again the third day from the dead, He ascended into heaven, sits on the right hand of God the Father almighty, from where He shall come to judge the living and the dead. At whose coming all men shall rise again with their bodies, and give an account for their own works: and them that have done good, shall go into life everlasting; and them that have done evil, into everlasting fire. This is the catholic faith, which everyone should believe faithfully.

The Nicene and Athanasian Creeds